CARTAGENA & COLOMBIA'S CARIBBEAN COAST

ANDREW DIER

Contents

CARTAGENA AND THE CARIBBEAN COAST

Colombia's Caribbean coast extends 1,760 kilometers (1,095 miles), from Venezuela to Panama, and is longer than California's coastline. The coastal area varies dramatically, with an astonishing array of landscapes: desolate deserts, snowcapped mountains, lowland swamps, dry savannahs, and rainforest. This region has so much to offer, it could easily be your only destination in Colombia.

© ANDREW DIER

HIGHLIGHTS

LOOK FOR ◖ TO FIND RECOMMENDED SIGHTS, ACTIVITIES, DINING, AND LODGING.

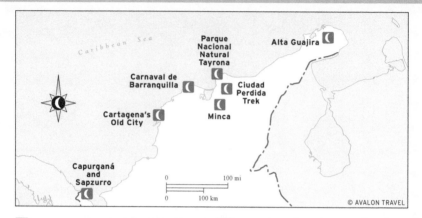

◖ **Cartagena's Old City:** Lose yourself in the romance of Cartagena's narrow streets and plazas, and cap off your day sipping a mojito atop the massive fortified walls (page 12).

◖ **Carnaval de Barranquilla:** Madcap and euphoric, this is Colombia's most famous celebration. Put on a costume and dance your way down the parade route (page 33).

◖ **Minca:** Take a break from the beach and chill in this refreshing town set in the foothills of the spectacular Sierra Nevada de Santa Marta mountains (page 44).

◖ **Parque Nacional Natural Tayrona:** Mountains meet jungles meet beaches at this popular national park near Santa Marta (page 46).

◖ **Ciudad Perdida Trek:** Climb the thousand-plus stone steps through the cloud forest to the mystical Lost City, the most important settlement of the Tayrona civilization (page 52).

◖ **Alta Guajira:** Be mesmerized by the stark beauty of desert landscapes, get to know Wayúu culture, and dine on fresh lobster at the top of South America (page 57).

◖ **Capurganá and Sapzurro:** Walk barefoot along deserted beaches, trek through dense rainforest among colorful frogs and howling monkeys, or cool off in a crystalline brook (page 65).

Cartagena is a majestic walled city full of magnificent churches and palaces, picturesque balcony-lined streets, and romantic plazas. Colombia's colonial past lives on in Mompox, a once-thriving port on the Río Magdalena where it feels as if time has stopped. The old city of Santa Marta has positioned itself as a great base from which to explore the beaches and mountains of the north-central coast.

Beach options abound here. The most famous are at Parque Nacional Natural Tayrona: glimmering golden sand beaches with the jungle backdrop of the Sierra Nevada. Islands in the Parque Nacional Natural Corales del Rosario y San Bernardo, between Tolú and Cartagena, beckon visitors with their white sandy beaches and five-star hotels.

There are many options for nature lovers. Minca, a small town located on the slopes of the

Sierra Nevada not far from Santa Marta, offers unparalleled bird-watching opportunities. In the jungles that envelop Capurganá and Sapzurro, you can go bird-watching, listen to the cries of howler monkeys, and count the colorful frogs you encounter along the many jungle paths in the area. Offshore, dive with the occasional sea turtle and observe myriad marine life in nearby waters.

Adventurous types can hike up to Ciudad Perdida in the Sierra Nevada. The views of the Lost City, with its eerie, beautiful terraces set atop the mountain, are simply unforgettable. Travel up the Guajira Peninsula, home of the Wayúu, Colombia's largest indigenous community. Here you'll find Cabo de la Vela, where the desert meets the sea, and stark, magnificent Punta Gallinas, the northernmost point in South America, where windswept dunes drop dramatically into Caribbean waters.

The Caribbean coast is vibrant with music and dance. It is the birthplace of *vallenato* (love ballads accompanied by accordion), which has European, African, and Amerindian roots. The coast is also home to many musical strains and dances with strong African rhythms, such as *cumbia,* a melodious traditional music once danced by African slaves, and *mapalé* and *champeta,* a more recent urban music born in Cartagena. The Carnaval de Baranquilla, declared a Masterpiece of the Intangible Heritage of Humanity by UNESCO, offers an unparalleled introduction to Caribbean music and folklore. Any time of year, Barranquilla's modern, interactive Museo del Caribe is an excellent overview of the people of the Caribbean and their very vibrant culture.

PLANNING YOUR TIME

There are a lot of sights to see in Cartagena. Take some time to wander the streets of the Old City and soak up the beauty and atmosphere. Two days will suffice, but three days is ideal. The coastal island of Barú or the Islas del Rosario archipelago can be done in an easy day or overnight trip.

From Cartagena, there are many possible excursions. Getting to the riverside town of Mompox involves five hours of travel by road and river, so staying two nights there is necessary. The seaside towns of Coveñas and Tolú are easy excursions with direct bus links from Cartagena. Barranquilla is an easy day or overnight trip.

Santa Marta is an excellent base for exploring the northern coast. If you prefer to be on the sea, the laid-back seaside village of Taganga, only a short ride from Santa Marta, could also be your base for exploration of the north.

Santa Marta offers many excursions. Spending a few days in the tranquil Sierra Nevada town of Minca is a welcome escape from the heat and an excellent base to explore the nearby mountains. The Parque Nacional Natural Tayrona is a possible day trip from Santa Marta or Taganga, but you will probably want to stay at least two nights to explore its beaches and jungles. The seaside resort of Palomino is just a 1.5-hour ride from Santa Marta. All of these towns make fine starting points for the four- to five-day trek to Ciudad Perdida, a must for any backpacker.

Most visitors to the Guajira Peninsula join an organized tour from Riohacha. From Riohacha it is possible to visit Cabo de la Vela via a bus to Uribia and then a ride in the back of a local passenger truck, but it will take several hours. Most tourists visit Cabo de la Vela as part of a tour of La Guajira. There is no transportation north of Cabo de la Vela, so you will need to join a tour to get to magnificent Punta Gallinas or to Parque Nacional Natural Macuira. Do not drive though the Guajira Peninsula without a guide: It is dangerous.

To the southwest of Cartagena, you'll find coastal communities Tolú and Coveñas and the untamed coastline of Córdoba, all easily accessed by bus from Cartagena or Montería. Medellín is the best gateway to the villages of Capurganá and Sapzurro on the Darien Gap. You could happily spend up to five days in this area.

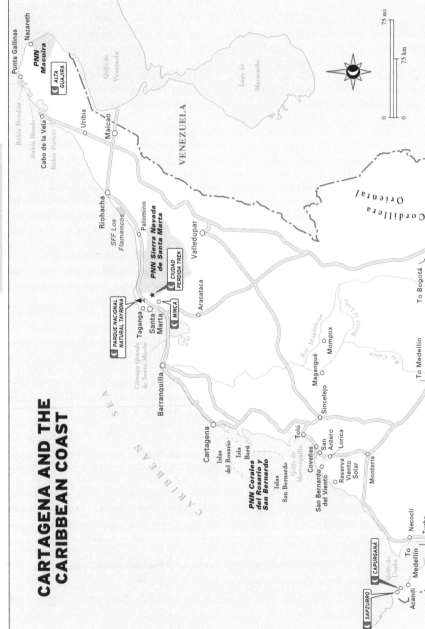

CARTAGENA AND THE CARIBBEAN COAST

© AVALON TRAVEL

Cartagena

Cartagena is unforgettable and magical, a highlight of any trip to Colombia. The main attraction is the Old City (Cartagena's *centro histórico*), which includes two districts: the Walled City (Ciudad Amurallada) and burgeoning Getsemaní. The magnificent walls of Ciudad Amurallada enclose narrow streets lined with magnificent *casas altas* (two-story houses that were home to wealthy merchants) with bougainvillea spilling out over their balconies. Getsemaní is an old working-class colonial neighborhood (also once enclosed by a wall) that today lures visitors with its many lodging, dining, and nightlife options. Near the Old City is the magnificent Castillo de San Felipe, one of the most impressive Spanish fortifications in the New World.

Outside the Old City, Cartagena is a large, poor, and sprawling city of almost one million people. If you want to get a sense of how big it is, visit La Popa for incredible views of the city and the bay. To get to know the real Cartagena first-hand, visit the frenetic Mercado de Bazurto and then, for contrast, take a stroll through high-end Bocagrande.

If you're looking to play at the beach, escape to the Islas del Rosario, as the beaches of Cartagena are unappealing.

History

Cartagena de Indias was founded in 1533 by Spanish conquistador Pedro de Heredia on a small Carib indigenous settlement. The city owes its glory to its strategic geographic position and

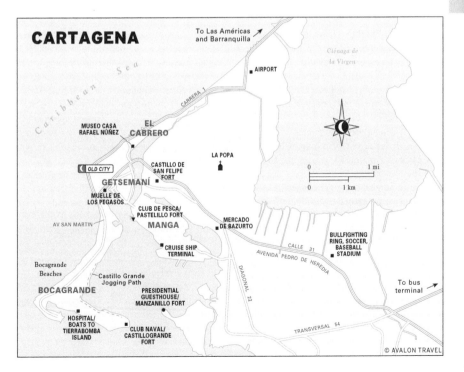

Cartagena's Old City

easily defended harbor. Heavily armed convoys of galleons sailed once a year from Spain to the New World, transporting agricultural and manufactured goods; on the way back they took on silver and gold from Peru and Mexico. The convoy's treasures were stored in Cartagena until the sail back to Spain.

The city proper was constructed at the north end of the large harbor, on a marshy island separated from the mainland. During the 16th century, the city was sacked by pirates numerous times, most notably by Sir Francis Drake in 1568. With the construction of fortifications, the city was spared major attacks. Castillo de San Felipe was built on the mainland to protect from an overland invasion. Pairs of forts were constructed at various passage points in the harbor to stop intruders. The construction of the fortifications took almost two centuries and was completed by mid-18th century.

With the construction of the Canal del Dique connecting Cartagena to the Río Magdalena in 1650, the city became the main entry port to Nueva Granada. The city also prospered as one of the main slave ports in Spanish America. It is estimated that more than one million slaves passed through the city. The Spanish crown forbade the enslavement of indigenous people, so plantation and mine owners bought African slaves, transported from Santo Domingo or West Africa. Conditions on and after the trip were horrendous. Slaves often escaped and created free communities known as *palenques,* such as the town of San Basilio, south of Cartagena.

During the fight for independence from Spain, Cartagena sided with the revolutionary movement. After Caracas, it was the second city in Nueva Granada to set up an independent junta, and it formally declared independence in 1812. In 1815, it was recaptured by the Spanish under the command of Pablo Murillo, after a siege that lasted more than three months. Cartagena was retaken by revolutionaries in 1821.

During the 19th century, Cartagena no longer enjoyed the activity and status it had as one of Spain's main ports. In the last decades of the century, Barranquilla eclipsed Cartagena as the main center of economic activity on the Caribbean coast. The economic decline had one good side effect: preserving the colonial past. The Old City remained largely intact through the 20th century, prompting UNESCO to declare it a World Heritage Site.

During the 20th century, Cartagena became a major industrial center and domestic tourist destination. In the past two decades, the city has received an estimated 100,000 displaced people, most fleeing violence in the Atlantic coast. The city has been unable to cope with this influx, and the result is a vast belt of shantytowns.

Cartagena remained relatively peaceful even during the worst periods of violence in the 1980s and 1990s, attracting tourists from across Colombia. In the past decade, Cartagena has become a major international tourist destination, with a proliferation of chic hotels in the Old City, glitzy Miami-style condominiums and hotels in Bocagrande, and new resorts along the coast north of the city. It boasts the Hay literary festival, a classical music festival, and an acclaimed film festival that attracts visitors from the world over.

Safety

All in all, the city is a safe place; however, the general precautions for all Colombian cities apply to Cartagena as well. Be careful while walking on the walls after dark. Police have an iffy reputation here, and have been known to stop and frisk young non-Colombian men in the evening, purportedly out of suspicion of drug possession, but in actuality they are looking for money. Some of the poor fishing villages on the islands nearby Cartagena are not safe to visit, at least not alone.

Orientation

Cartagena is located on the Caribbean coast of Colombia about 130 kilometers (80 miles) southwest of Barranquilla and over 1,100 kilometers (680 miles) north of Bogotá. The city is at the north end of a large bay with the same name.

The focal point of Cartagena is the Old City, known as the *centro histórico,* or simply El Centro. The Old City is the original Spanish settlement completely enclosed by a massive stone wall. The Walled City is set out in a fairly regular grid with numerous plazas. The streets here have names that change from block to block; no one really knows them or uses them. Find your way by identifying the main squares—Torre de los Coches, Plaza de la Aduana, Plaza de Santo Domingo, Plaza de Bolívar, and Plaza Fernandez de Madrid—and making your way from one to the other. It takes some practice, but walking the charming streets of the Old City is a pleasure.

Historically, the main entrance to the Walled City was the gate where the Torre del Reloj (clock tower) now stands. Just south is the Bahía de las Ánimas and the Muelle de los Pegasos, from which point tourist boats to the Islas del Rosario depart.

During colonial times, the poorer district of Getsemaní was a separate island connected by bridge to the Old City. In the late 19th and early 20th centuries, the mangroves and marshes were filled in.

Southeast of Getsemaní is La Matuna, a busy commercial center full of 20th-century high-rises. To the east is the massive Castillo de San Felipe and farther on is La Popa, the only significant hill in Cartagena. East of La Popa is Mercado de Bazurto, Cartagena's huge central market, which is on Avenida Pedro de Heredia, the main road that leads to the bus terminal and out of the city.

Just north of the Old City is the 19th-century district of El Cabrero, where the villa of former president Rafael Núñez, today the Casa Museo Rafael Núñez, is located. Farther north are the residential neighborhoods of Marbella and Crespo, where the airport is. About two kilometers farther north, next to the fishing village of La Boquilla, is the seaside development of Las Américas.

South of the Old City is Bocagrande, with its many high-rise hotels and residential buildings. It was first developed in the 1960s and 1970s as a domestic tourist destination. It is the stomping ground of Cartagena's rich residents. Since around 2005, however, there has been a spurt of construction of high-end, Miami Beach-inspired white

typical street in Cartagena

residential skyscrapers. The main attractions here are the beaches. They are very popular on weekends. (There's even a gay-ish beach at the very end known as Hollywood.) But they're just OK. The sand is gray, and there's a constant stream of persistent vendors and masseuses.

The peninsula of Castillo Grande on the bay side of Bocagrande is an upscale residential neighborhood. The sidewalk that wraps around it makes for a pleasant stroll or place to jog.

SIGHTS
⟨ Old City
LAS MURALLAS

Referring to Cartagena's *murallas* (walls), Colombians endearingly call the city "El Corralito de Piedra" (little stone corral). These walls are one of the most salient features of the city. After Drake sacked the city in 1568, the Spanish started fortifying access to the bay and the perimeter wall around the city. The effort took almost two centuries to complete. The walls that can be seen today are mostly from the 17th and 18th centuries.

The most impressive part of the wall is the stretch that runs parallel to the sea. This includes three *baluartes* (bulwarks, or ramparts) where Spaniards stood ready to defend the city from attack. The massive Baluartes de San Lucas y de Santa Catalina, built in the very north of the city to repel attacks from land, are known as Las Tenazas because they are shaped like pincers. When the sea started depositing sediments and expanding the seashore, thus enabling the enemy to maneuver south along the wall, the Spanish built a spike to halt them. This defensive structure, known as El Espigón de la Tenaza, is now home to the Museo de las Fortificaciones (Baluarte de Santa Catalina, tel. 5/656-0591, www.fortificacionesdecartagena.com, 8am-6pm daily, COP$7,000). At the westernmost tip of the walls, facing the sea, is the equally impressive Baluarte Santo Domingo, now home to Café del Mar. At the southern tip of the segment of walls facing the sea, next to the Plaza Santa Teresa, are the Baluartes de San Ignacio y de San Francisco Javier, also home to a pleasant outdoor bar.

A *paseo* (walk) on the walls is the quintessential Cartagena late-afternoon experience, enjoyed by international visitors, Colombian honeymooners, and Cartagenan high school students still in their school uniforms. The best time for this promenade is around 5pm. In the evenings, vacationers head to the handful of bars for a pre- or post-dinner drink. Avoid strolling the wall late at night, especially alone.

CLAUSTRO AND IGLESIA SAN PEDRO CLAVER

The Claustro San Pedro Claver (Plaza de San Pedro Claver No. 30-01, tel. 5/664-4991, 8am-5:30pm Mon.-Fri., 8am-4:30pm Sat.-Sun., COP$9,000) is an old Jesuit monastery, now museum, where Pedro Claver served as a priest. He is known for his compassion towards newly arrived African slaves, and is said to have baptized thousands of them. For his dedication to slaves, the priest was the first person to be canonized in the New World. The museum has relics and art from the colonial era and sometimes hosts temporary exhibitions. You can visit the small quarters where San Pedro Claver lived and climb up to the choir balcony of the Iglesia de San Pedro Claver. The cloister has a three-story courtyard brimming with flowers and trees.

Adjacent to the monastery is the Iglesia de San Pedro Claver (Plaza de San Pedro Claver No. 30-01, tel. 5/664-4991, masses 6:45am and 6pm Mon.-Sat., 7am, 10am, noon, and 6pm Sun.), which is adorned by a beautiful marble altar and is the final resting place for San Pedro Claver.

MUSEO DE ARTE MODERNO DE CARTAGENA DE INDIAS

Cartagena's main art museum, the Museo de Arte Moderno de Cartagena de Indias (Cl. 30 No. 4-08, Plaza de San Pedro Claver, tel. 5/664-5815, 9am-noon and 3pm-6pm Mon.-Fri., 10am-1pm Sat., COP$5,000, Tues. free) is on the square in front of the San Pedro Claver plaza, which is filled with several metallic sculptures by Cartagenero Edgardo Carmona that depict quotidian scenes of

Cartagena life. The museum has a small permanent collection of works from 20th-century Colombian artists, including native sons Alejandro Obregón and Enrique Grau. The museum is in the old Customs House.

MUSEO NAVAL DEL CARIBE

Adjoining the rear of the Iglesia de San Pedro Claver is the Museo Naval del Caribe (Cl. 31 No. 3-62, Cl. San Juan de Dios, tel. 5/664-2440, www.museonavaldelcaribe.com, 10am-5:30pm daily, COP$7,000). This museum provides a history lesson of the earliest indigenous dwellers who lived in the area, continuing through the Spanish conquest and including a bit about the many (mostly English) pirates who tried to steal the Spaniards' gold loot, which they had absconded with from all across South America. The second floor has a lot of replicas of grand ships from the period and a history of the Colombian navy (you may be surprised to learn of its participation in the Korean War). There are few explanations in English. Part of the building dates to the 17th century and was a Jesuit convent; after they were expelled by the king, it was converted into a hospital.

PLAZA DE BOLÍVAR

One of the city's most pleasant squares is the Plaza de Bolívar, once used for bullfights. It was transformed into a park in the late 19th century. With a statue of Simón Bolívar in the center, nearly always with a disrespectful pigeon resting upon his head, this shady spot is very inviting.

CATEDRAL BASÍLICA MENOR

Diagonal to the Plaza de Bolívar is the built-to-last Catedral Basílica Menor (tel. 5/664-7283, masses 10am-noon Mon.-Sat., 8am, noon, and 7pm Sun., COP$13,000, free during masses). It was built in the 16th century and doubled as a fortress. It was attacked by Sir Francis Drake in 1586. The facade, along with most of the interior, has been stripped of the Italianate stucco exterior that was added in the 20th century and restored to its former austere stone look. The cathedral's pale orange belltower,

CARTAGENA

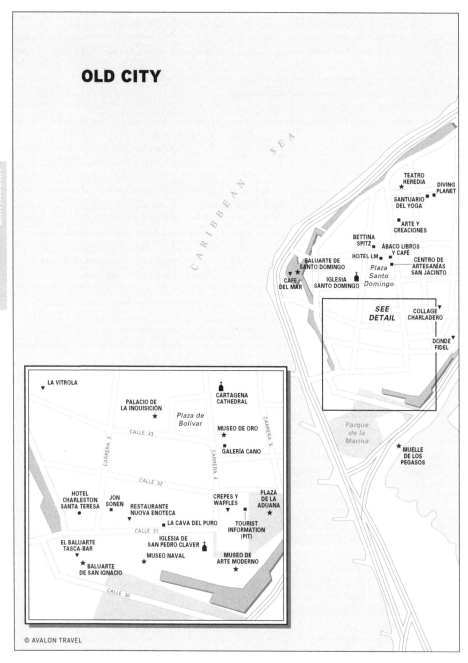

OLD CITY

CARIBBEAN SEA

TEATRO HEREDIA
DIVING PLANET
SANTUARIO DEL YOGA
ARTE Y CREACIONES
BETTINA SPITZ
ÁBACO LIBROS Y CAFÉ
HOTEL LM
CENTRO DE ARTESANÍAS SAN JACINTO
BALUARTE DE SANTO DOMINGO
Plaza Santo Domingo
CAFE DEL MAR
IGLESIA SANTO DOMINGO
SEE DETAIL
COLLAGE CHARLADERO
DONDE FIDEL

Parque de la Marina

LA VITROLA

PALACIO DE LA INQUISICIÓN
CARTAGENA CATHEDRAL
Plaza de Bolívar
MUSEO DE ORO
GALERÍA CANO
CALLE 33
CARRERA 3
CARRERA 4
CARRERA 5

CALLE 32

HOTEL CHARLESTON SANTA TERESA
JON SONEN
RESTAURANTE NUOVA ENOTECA
CREPES Y WAFFLES
PLAZA DE LA ADUANA
LA CAVA DEL PURO
TOURIST INFORMATION (PIT)
CALLE 31

EL BALUARTE TASCA-BAR
IGLESIA DE SAN PEDRO CLAVER
MUSEO NAVAL
MUSEO DE ARTE MODERNO
BALUARTE DE SAN IGNACIO

CALLE 30

MUELLE DE LOS PEGASOS

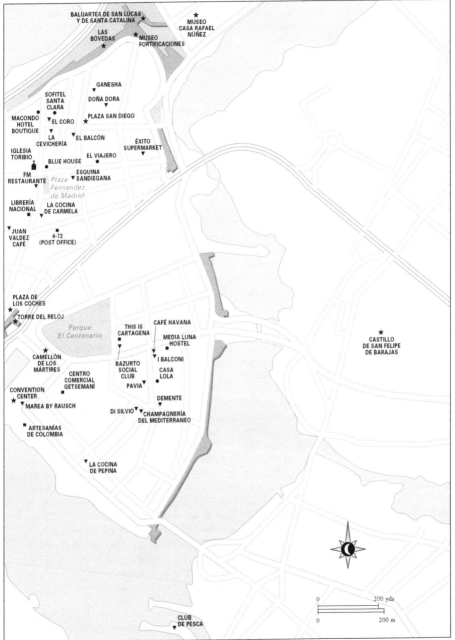

BALUARTES DE SAN LUCAS
Y DE SANTA CATALINA

MUSEO
CASA RAFAEL
NÚÑEZ

LAS
BÓVEDAS

MUSEO
FORTIFICACIONES

GANESHA

SOFITEL
SANTA
CLARA

DOÑA DORA

MACONDO
HOTEL
BOUTIQUE

EL CORO

PLAZA SAN DIEGO

LA
CEVICHERÍA

EL BALCÓN

ÉXITO
SUPERMARKET

IGLESIA
TORIBIO

EL VIAJERO

BLUE HOUSE

FM
RESTAURANTE

ESQUINA
SANDIEGANA

Plaza
Fernandez
de Madrid

LIBRERÍA
NACIONAL

LA COCINA
DE CARMELA

JUAN
VALDEZ
CAFÉ

4-72
(POST OFFICE)

PLAZA DE
LOS COCHES

TORRE DEL RELOJ

Parque
El Centenario

THIS IS
CARTAGENA

CAFÉ HAVANA

MEDIA LUNA
HOSTEL

CASTILLO
DE SAN FELIPE
DE BARAJAS

CAMELLÓN
DE LOS
MÁRTIRES

CENTRO
COMERCIAL
GETSEMANÍ

BAZURTO
SOCIAL
CLUB

I BALCONI

CASA
LOLA

PAVIA

CONVENTION
CENTER

DEMENTE

MAREA BY RAUSCH

DI SILVIO

CHAMPAGNERÍA
DEL MEDITERRANEO

ARTESANÍAS
DE COLOMBIA

LA COCINA
DE PEPINA

200 yds

200 m

CLUB
DE PESCA

CARTAGENA

which dates to the early 20th century, can be seen across the Old City. Stroll the ornate cathedral during or before a mass to visit for free. Audio guides are available 8am-6pm daily.

PALACIO DE LA INQUISICIÓN

On the south side of the plaza is the Palacio de la Inquisición (Cl. 34 No. 3-11, Plaza de Bolívar, tel. 5/664-4570, 9am-6pm Mon.-Sat., 10am-4pm Sun., COP$15,000). This remarkable 18th-century construction, one of the finest examples of colonial architecture in Cartagena standing today, was the headquarters of the Spanish Inquisition in Cartagena. In this building was housed the Tribunal del Santo Oficio, whose purpose was to exert control over the Indians, mestizos, and African slaves not only in Nueva Granada but also in New World colonies in Central America, the Caribbean, and Venezuela. The tribunal was active from 1610 until the late 17th century. There were two other tribunals in the New World: one in Lima and another in Mexico City.

The first floor of the building is a museum displaying the weapons of torture employed by authorities as part of the Inquisition. In Cartagena as elsewhere, the most common punishable crime was "witchcraft," and hundreds of supposed heretics (indigenous people were excluded from punishment) were condemned here. On the second floor are exhibition spaces dedicated to the restoration of the building and to the history of Cartagena. Most explanations are written in Spanish; you may decide to hire one of the English-speaking guides (COP$35,000 for a group up to five persons). On your way out, take a right and then another right onto the Calle de la Inquisición and look for a small window on the palace wall. This was a secret spot where citizens of colonial Cartagena could anonymously report others for various and sundry heresies.

MUSEO DEL ORO ZENÚ

The Museo del Oro Zenú (Cra. 4 No. 33-26, Plaza de Bolívar, tel. 5/660-0778, 10am-1pm and 3pm-7pm Tues.-Fri., 10am-1pm and 2pm-5pm Sat., 11am-4pm Sun., free), on the north side of the Plaza de Bolívar, exhibits gold jewelry and funerary objects from the Zenú indigenous people, who were the original dwellers of the Río Magdalena area and Río Sinú valley, to the southwest of Cartagena. It has excellent Spanish and English explanations. A smaller version of the Museo del Oro in Bogotá, this museum has a regional focus and is one of the few tributes to indigenous culture today in Cartagena.

CASA MUSEO RAFAEL NÚÑEZ

Just beyond the wall in the Cabrero neighborhood is the Casa Museo Rafael Núñez (Calle Real del Cabrero, tel. 5/664-5305, 9am-5:30pm Tues.-Sun., COP$10,000). This is the house of Rafael Núñez, the four-time former president of Colombia, author of the 1886 Colombian constitution, and author of the 11 verses of Colombia's national anthem. Núñez governed Colombia from this, his coastal home. The museum, which underwent a renovation in 2013, has memorabilia from his political life and is a beautiful example of 19th-century Cartagena architecture. Núñez was born and died in Cartagena, and he lies at rest in the Ermita de Nuestra Señora de las Mercedes across the street.

Castillo de San Felipe

The largest Spanish fort in the New World, the magnificent Castillo de San Felipe (Cerro de San Lázaro, east of Old City, 8am-6pm daily, COP$17,000) must have given pirates pause as they contemplated an attack on the city. It was built atop the Cerro de San Lázaro outside of the Walled City to repel attacks by land. Construction was begun in 1639 and completed over a century later. It was never captured. Tunnels enabled soldiers to quickly move about without being noticed, and cells housed the occasional unlucky prisoner.

Today, visitors ramble through tunnels and secret passageways (a flashlight will come in quite handy), and views from the highest points of the fort are magnificent.

The best time to visit the fort is in the late afternoon, when the intense sun abates. Audio tours

© ANDREW DIER

The monolithic Castillo de San Felipe is one of the most impressive Spanish forts in the New World.

(COP$10,000) are available. For many, the view of the fort from a distance suffices, especially at nighttime when it is lit up. If you want to do things up for a special celebration, you can rent out the entire *castillo* (fireworks are an additional charge!). Contact the Sociedad de Mejoras Públicas de Cartagena (Castillo de San Felipe de Barajas, tel. 5/656-0590, www.fortificacionesdecartagena.com) for more information.

To get there, take a bus from Avenida Santander (COP$1,500). You can also walk from the Old City, though maneuvering through and around traffic is not fun. A taxi will cost COP$5,000.

La Popa

La Popa is a 150-meter-high (500-foot-high) hill east of the Castillo de San Felipe, so named because of its resemblance to a ship's stern (*popa* in Spanish). La Popa is home to the Convento Nuestra Señora de la Candelaria (Cra. 20A 29D-16, tel. 5/666-0976, 9am-5:30pm daily, COP$5,000), which was built by Augustinian monks, reportedly on a pagan site of worship. The monastery has a lovely courtyard, a small chapel where faithful pray to the Virgen de la Candelaria, and memorabilia from Pope John Paul II's visit to the monastery in 1986. Most tourists come here for the views over Cartagena and out to the sea. You can take a taxi there from the Old City for COP$50,000-60,000 round-trip. Arrange the price in advance and make sure the driver will wait for you there.

Sightseeing Tours

The folks at This Is Cartagena (Av. Centenario No. 30-42, tel. 5/660-0969, www.ticartagena.com, 9am-6pm Mon.-Fri., COP$115,000) offer two tours of the city. One is a full city tour (about four hours) that hits all the major sights, from La Popa to the beaches of Bocagrande. It's the comfortable way to see the city: in an air-conditioned vehicle. Entries to all the sights are included in the tour price. The second tour is a walking tour of the Old City, in which you'll learn a lot about this fascinating

Plaza to Plaza Walking Tour

© ANDREW DIER

the Iglesia Santo Toribio, one of Cartagena's beautiful colonial churches

CARTAGENA

The best way to get to know Cartagena is to go for a morning stroll, finding your way from plaza to plaza, and even getting lost a couple of times.

Start at the Plaza de los Coches (opposite Getsemaní), once the main entry point to the city. It is easily identifiable by the iconic 19th-century Torre del Reloj (clock tower) that tops the entrance though the wall. Inside stands a statue of Cartagena's founder Pedro de Heredia. During the colonial period, this plaza was the site of the city's slave market. During much of the 20th century it bustled with commercial activity. Today, the plaza is filled with watering holes catering to visitors.

Immediately to the southwest is the large triangular Plaza de la Aduana, once the seat of power in colonial Cartagena. It is surrounded by stately colonial mansions. A statue of Christopher Columbus presides in the center. It's also got a fair share of ATMs and is where the main tourist office is located.

Adjacent to the southeast is the Plaza de San Pedro, a small square located in front of the towering Iglesia de San Pedro Claver and attached convent where Saint Peter Claver, a Jesuit monk dedicated to succoring African slaves, ministered.

Walking two blocks north on Calle de San Pedro you'll arrive at the city's heart, the leafy Plaza de Bolívar, a shady park with benches, fountains, and a statue of Simón Bolívar in the middle. It is surrounded by some of the most important buildings of the city, including the Catedral Basílica Menor and the Palacio de la Inquisición.

On Calle de los Santos de Piedra and Calle de Nuestra Señora del Rosario is the Plaza de Santo Domingo, heart of the former upper class quarter. You will notice many superb two-story *casas altas* built by rich merchants. The plaza is dominated by the austere Iglesia de Santo Domingo. A rotund nude bronze sculpture by Fernando Botero, live musical performances, and many outdoor cafés liven up the popular plaza.

Next is the large, green Plaza Fernández de Madrid in the historic working class San Diego district. On one side is the charming Iglesia Santo Toribio with its magnificent wooden ceiling and cannonball damage (compliments of English pirate Edward Vernon).

On Calle Cochera del Hobo is the tiny Plaza San Diego, which is surrounded by inviting restaurants. It's also where you can join the locals who gather around Doña Dora's food stall. This is the place to sample a *carimañola* and *arepa de huevo*, two deep-fried and totally delicious treats.

End your roaming at the Plaza de las Bóvedas at the extreme northwest of the city. Once the location of a military storehouse, this is where you can load up on handicrafts at the Galería de las Bóvedas.

city, its history, architecture, and people. This Is Cartagena offers several other tours, including day trips to the Islas de Rosario, a photography tour, and even a "historic drinking tour."

ENTERTAINMENT AND EVENTS

Nightlife

La Esquina Sandiegana (corner of Cl. del Santísimo and Cl. de los Púntales, 5pm-2am Sun.-Thurs., 5pm-3am Fri.-Sat., no cover) is a locals' place, where the music is salsa and the drink is beer. Its walls are decorated with salsa posters, album covers, and photographs of salsa greats. It's a hole-in-the-wall bar in the San Diego neighborhood.

Bazurto Social Club (Av. del Centenario Cra. 9 No. 30-42, tel. 5/664-3124, www.bazurtosocialclub.com, 7pm-3am Thurs.-Sat., cover varies) is an always-lively restaurant-bar, popular with Colombians and international visitors alike. Get a taste for Afro-Colombian *champeta* beats, as live acts, including the Bazurto All Stars, often perform here. They also serve food, such as shrimp empanadas and paella. The house drink is the fruity rum *machacos*.

The former site of a convent, El Coro (Cl. del Torno No. 39-29, tel. 5/650-4700, 5pm-2am Sun.-Thurs., 5pm-3am Fri.-Sat., no cover), at the Hotel Santa Clara, is an inviting, if posh, spot for an after-dinner drink. From Wednesday to Sunday, live music, with a nod to Havana, is on offer until late. How many places can you enjoy Latin jazz while downing mojitos in a former convent?

Café Havana (intersection of Cl. de la Media Luna and Cl. del Guerrero, cell tel. 314/556-3905 or 310/610-2324, www.cafehavanacartagena.com, 8:30pm-4am Thurs.-Sat., cover varies) famously got the endorsement of former Secretary of State Hillary Clinton on her trip to Colombia in 2012. It's a place for rum drinks and dancing. Café Havana is open Sundays when the following Monday is a holiday.

Donde Fidel (Plaza de los Coches, tel. 5/664-3127, noon-2am Sun.-Thurs., noon-3am Fri.-Sat., no cover) is a tiny salsa-lovers' spot where the action spills out onto the plaza in front. Good times and cold beer can be found here.

You've walked atop the massive walls of the Old City, and now it's time for some drinks. A sundown drink, with the Caribbean breeze kissing your face on the *murallas* (walls), is a Cartagena experience that shouldn't be missed. There are three options. First, the Baluarte Tasca-Bar (Cl. San Juan de Dios, tel. 5/660-0468, www.baluartesanfranciscojavier.com, 5:30pm-2am daily, no cover) is an open-air restaurant-bar at the northwesternmost corner of the wall, across from the Plaza de Santa Teresa. It's chilled out here, not trendy (but the drink prices are on the steep side: COP$24,000 for a margarita). The most happening spot would be, without a doubt, the Café del Mar (tel. 5/664-6513, 5pm-3am daily, no cover), on the wall near the Plaza de Santo Domingo entrance. Here the music is loungey and electronic, and it stays busy until late. It's spread out atop the wall, making it hard to mingle with others or even to carry on much of a conversation. But the drinks will quench your thirst and the music is seductive. The third wall option is to go rogue: hang out on the wall, drink an Águila beer sold by a roaming vendor, and listen to the music emanating from Café del Mar.

Wednesdays are the new Saturdays in Cartagena. In Getsemaní, Visa por un Sueño (Media Luna Hostel, Cl. de la Media Luna No. 10-46, tel. 5/664-0639, 9pm-3am Wed., COP$10,000) is a weekly party held on the rooftop of the Media Luna Hostel that has become Cartagena's most famous soiree, when backpackers mix it up with Colombians. Get there early—this party gets packed.

Festivals and Events

Cartagena feels like a celebration all the time, but especially November to February, when an array of cultural events are featured.

HAY FESTIVAL

Hay Festival (www.hayfestival.com) is an important international festival that began in Wales nearly 30 years ago. It celebrates literature, music, environmental awareness, and community and is held in various cities across the world, including in Cartagena in late January. Bill Clinton has called it the "Woodstock of the mind." In addition to talks and concerts, the festival holds educational programs for youth in the neighborhoods of Cartagena. It also provides free or discounted tickets to students. Most of the events take place in the Teatro Heredia (Cl. de la Chichería No. 38-10, tel. 5/664-6023 or 5/664-9631). While the festival's name is pronounced as the English "hay," in Colombia it's often pronounced as the Spanish "*hay*" ("ai"). Hay Festival is thus a double entendre: *hay festival* in Spanish means yes, there is a festival!

FESTIVAL INTERNACIONAL DE MÚSICA

Over the course of a week in early to mid-January, the churches, plazas, and theaters of the Walled City become the setting for classical music concerts by musicians from all over the world during the Festival Internacional de Música (International Music Festival, www.cartagenamusicfestival.com, tickets www.tuboleta.com). Most concerts sell out far in advance, but if you can't get tickets, you might be able to catch a free performance in one of the churches or plazas in the Old City.

FESTIVAL INTERNACIONAL DE CINE DE CARTAGENA DE INDIAS

If you're in town during late February and are looking for an excuse to escape the heat, here it is: the Festival Internacional de Cine de Cartagena de Indias (International Film Festival, tel. 5/664-2345, www.ficcifestival.com). A tradition since the 1960s, this week-long film festival has an interesting program of documentaries, Colombian films, and shorts; a series of roundtable discussions with prominent actors and directors; and educational activities in neighborhoods throughout the city. The venues include historic buildings and plazas.

CONCURSO NACIONAL DE BELLEZA

Beauty contests, and especially the Concurso Nacional de Belleza (Miss Colombia Pageant, tel. 5/660-0779, www.srtacolombia.org), are a big deal in Colombia. The coronation of Señorita Colombia takes place every November and is the highlight of Cartagena's Independence Day celebrations. Aspirers for the title represent each of the departments of the country, in addition to some cities. Ladies from the Valle del Cauca and Atlántico have won the most titles (10 each) since the pageant began in the 1930s. In 2001, the first Miss Colombia of Afro-Colombian heritage was chosen: Vanessa Mendoza, who represented the Chocó department. Tickets to the main events—the swimsuit competition at the Cartagena Hilton and the coronation at the Centro de Convenciones—are hard to come by but not impossible to purchase.

ELECTRONIC MUSIC FESTIVALS

In early January every year, especially on the first weekend after New Year's Day, one or two big beachside electronic music festivals take place. The most well-known and regular festival is Ultra Mar, but there are others. These parties are often the main reason the under-35 crowd from Bogotá, Medellín, and Cali converges on the city during the New Year's holidays. Tickets and information can be found at Tu Boleta (www.tuboleta.com). Double-check before heading out to one of these events, as sometimes the location changes at the last minute.

SHOPPING
Shopping Centers and Malls

The bazaar-like Centro Comercial Getsemaní (Cl. 30 No. 8B-74, tel. 5/664-2508, hours vary daily) shopping center doesn't really cater to tourists. It's made up of hundreds of small mom-and-pop kiosks that sell just about anything: computer supplies, notebooks, beauty supplies, handicrafts, and knickknacks. You can probably get your nails done here as well.

Centro Comercial Caribe Plaza (Pie de la Popa, Cl. 29D No. 22-108, tel. 5/669-2332, 10am-8pm Mon.-Thurs., 10am-9pm Fri.-Sun.) is an upscale modern mall near the Castillo de San Felipe

© ANDREW DIER

fresh fish at the Mercado de Bazurto

with numerous clothing and shoe stores, movie theaters, and a food court.

MERCADO DE BAZURTO

Definitely not for the faint of heart, a visit to the sprawling, grimy Mercado de Bazurto (Av. Pedro Heredia, 5am-4pm daily) is the best way to connect with the real Cartagena. On the periphery of the market be sure to peruse the seafood area, where women sell the catch of the day to restaurant owners. Be amazed at all the different kinds of fruit on offer. To get to the market, take a bus from Avenida Santander (COP$1,500) or a taxi (COP$7,000 from the Old City).

Another way of visiting the market is the Mercado de Bazurto Tour (tel. 5/660-1492, cell tel. 315/655-4120, cevicheria@hotmail.com, COP$250,000 pp), organized by Jorge Escandón, the owner of La Cevichería and Bazurto Social Club. On the tour, you'll learn about the ingredients that make Caribbean cuisine special, particularly the seafood and exotic fruits. You'll also meet the vendors who have worked their entire lives behind a stall at the market. Afterwards you'll head to a beach house and have a gourmet lunch featuring lobster and other delicacies prepared by Jorge and his staff.

Handicrafts

The most historic place to pick up some Colombian handicrafts is at Las Bóvedas (extreme northeastern corner of the wall, 9am-6pm daily). Once a military storehouse, today it's the place to buy multicolored hammocks and all kinds of Colombian *artesanías* of varying quality.

For high quality handicrafts you're better off going to Artesanías de Colombia (Centro de Convenciones, Local 5, tel. 5/660-9615, 10am-7pm Mon.-Sat.). This is a government entity whose mission it is to promote Colombian handicrafts and craftspeople. This store sells handicrafts from across the country but specializes in masks from the Carnaval de Barranquilla, woven *mochilas* (handbags) from indigenous groups in the Sierra Nevada, and the colorful embroidery of *molas* from indigenous groups in the Darien Gap region near Panama.

Jewelry

Colombian emeralds are considered to be some of the finest in the world. Many jewelers in the Centro Histórico sell emerald jewelry and can custom make jewelry for you. One of the most highly regarded jewelers is Galería Cano (Plaza Bolívar No. 33-20, Local 679, tel. 5/664-7078, www.galeriacano.com.co, 9am-7pm Mon.-Fri., 10am-7pm Sat.). They specialize in gold, silver, and emerald jewelry. Cano has other locations in the airport and at the Hotel Santa Clara, as well as in Bogotá.

Cigars

In Cartagena, touches of Cuba are found everywhere: mojitos, music, and, too, the cigars. At La Cava del Puro (Cl. de las Damas No. 3-106, tel. 5/664-9482, www.lacavadelpuro.com, 9am-8pm Mon.-Sat., 10am-8pm Sun.) they don't sell just any old stogie; here the cigars come from Havana and are of the best quality. Smoking is not only permitted here, but in fact promoted. Sometimes a little whiskey is even served to perusing clients. Note that cigars with labels that say "Hecho in Cuba" may be confiscated by customs agents upon arrival in the United States. Cigars that come from the Barichara area in the Colombian department of Santander are quite good and much cheaper, and you can take them across borders with no questions asked.

Clothing

Along Calle Santo Domingo there are several boutiques of top Colombian designers. Bogotana Bettina Spitz (Cl. de la Mantilla No. 3-37, tel. 5/660-2160, www.bettinaspitz.com, 11am-1pm and 2pm-8pm daily) sells casual, beach, and formal clothes for women, as well as an array of accessories, shoes, and some men's items. Jon Sonen (Cl. Ricaurte No. 31-56, tel. 5/664-1092 or 5/660-4682, www.jonsonen.com, 10am-8pm Sun.-Thurs., 10am-9pm Fri.-Sat.) is a Colombian label specializing in menswear, with stores throughout the country.

You'll notice that guayabera shirts are what men wear around Cartagena, to restaurants and events. It's possible to spend a fortune on them, but if you want to blend in without busting your budget, go to Arte y Creaciones (Cl. Don Sancho No. 36-94, cell tel. 320/583-9091, noon-8pm Mon.-Fri., 10am-8pm Sat.-Sun.), where a cotton guayabera will run you about COP$55,000. Another option for cheap guayaberas is Centro de Artesanías de San Jacinto (Cl. de la Iglesia No. 35-59, tel. 5/660-1574, 9am-8:30pm daily).

Books

Abaco Libros (Cl. 36 No. 3-86, Cl. de la Mantilla, tel. 5/664-8290, 9am-9pm Mon.-Sat., 3pm-9pm Sun.) is a small book shop/café with a variety of books on Cartagena, top Colombian novels, and a selection of magazines, classics, and best sellers in English. Librería Nacional (Cl. Segunda de Badillo No. 36-27, tel. 5/664-1448, 8:30am-12:30pm and 2pm-6:30pm Mon.-Fri., 8:30am-5pm Sat.) is a chain bookstore with shelves full of Colombian and Spanish-language books, but not much in the way of books in English.

SPORTS AND RECREATION

If you're looking for a place to jog or stroll, the bayside path along the peninsula of Castillo Grande (Cra. 5 from Clls. 6-10 and along Cl. 6 from Cras. 6-14) in the Bocagrande sector is very nice, particularly in the late afternoon. From here you'll have great views of the Cartagena port and La Popa in the far distance. Forming an L shape, the path is about two kilometers long.

Biking

The best time to explore Cartagena by bike is early on a Sunday morning or on a Sunday or Monday evening when there is little activity and no traffic in the Old City. Pato Bikes (Cl. de la Media Luna, Cra. 8B No. 25-110, tel. 5/664-0639, cell tel. 301/423-9996, 9pm-9pm daily, COP$20,000) and Bike Route (Callejón de los Estribos No. 2-78, cell tel. 318/456-1392, 10am-11pm daily, COP$5,000/hour, COP$30,000/day) are both located in Getsemaní and rent bikes. In addition to bike rental, Bicitour Getsemaní (Cl. Carretero, Getsemaní, cell tel. 300/357-1825, COP$5,000/2-hour rental) offers guided tours of the Old City on two wheels. Many hostels and some hotels also have bicycles for hire.

Diving

Diving Planet (Cl. Estanco del Aguardiente No. 5-94, tel. 5/664-2171, www.divingplanet.org, 8am-7pm Mon.-Sat.) offers classes and diving excursions to some 25 locations throughout the Parque Nacional Natural Corales del Rosario y San Bernardo. A one-day mini-course with two immersions costs COP$305,000. A day trip with two immersions for those who are certified divers costs COP$290,000. If you pay in advance on their webpage or pay in cash once in Cartagena you'll receive a discount. Multiple day PADI certification courses are also available. Some of these plans include an overnight on the white beaches of the Islas del Rosario. Snorkeling excursions are also available (COP$190,000).

Yoga

Santuario del Yoga (Cl. El Estanco del Aguardiente No. 5, tel. 5/668-5338, cell tel. 313/649-3133, 8:30am-5pm daily, COP$15,000 per class) offers yoga classes in a small studio in the Walled City and also classes on the beach on occasion. Some instructors are bilingual.

ACCOMMODATIONS

Cartagena remains the top tourist destination in Colombia (and is second only to Bogotá in terms of international arrivals), and the crowds keep coming. Hotel options have flourished since 2000. The Old City and Getsemaní have become a favorite location for high-end boutique hotels. At the other end of the spectrum, hostels have begun to appear in these same neighborhoods. Finding a good mid-range option, however, is a challenge.

A short bus or taxi ride away from colonial Cartagena is its version of Miami Beach: Bocagrande. Large high-rise hotels facing the waters of the Caribbean are the norm. This area is popular with Colombian tourists. There are some midrange and budget options here, though not with a view to the sea.

For those interested in beaches, the Las Américas area two kilometers past the airport is home to many new, large high-rise hotels. Finally, there are lodging options in the Islas de Rosario. Spending a night there may be more satisfying, albeit much more expensive, than a day trip.

Peak tourist seasons in Cartagena are during the last week of November (which is when the city celebrates its independence from Spain and hosts the Miss Colombia beauty pageant), from mid-December to mid-January, Semana Santa (Holy Week) in March or April, June-July during school vacations, and during any of the long weekends when Monday is a holiday (check a Colombian calendar). Cartagena is at its liveliest (and more fun) when the out-of-towners converge on it, particularly during the end-of-year

holidays when it's two to three weeks of celebration. But finding a place to stay may be difficult, as room rates spike.

Old City and Getsemaní
UNDER COP$70,000

The Shangri-La of backpacker hostels in Cartagena is the famous **Media Luna** (Cl. de la Media Luna No. 10-46, tel. 5/664-3423, www.medialunahostel.com, COP$37,000 dorm). Located on the edge of Getsemaní, it's a high-energy kind of place with multicultural socializing (and flirting) centered on the small pool in the courtyard. If you're looking to break out of your shell, this may be the place. It has a capacity of over 100 with just a couple of private rooms (book early for those). There's a burrito place attached to the Luna, they organize lots of activities, and bikes are available to rent. Then there's the bar: On Wednesday nights, turn up on the early side (around 9pm) to squeeze in at their famous Visa por un Sueño party. This hostel isn't the best place for travelers over the age of 28.

In the Old City, the Uruguayan hostel chain **El Viajero** (Cl. Siete Infantes No. 9-45, tel. 5/660-2598, www.elviajerohostels.com, COP$30,000 dorm, COP$75,000 pp d) has air-conditioned dorm rooms of various sizes and a handful of private rooms, which are located across the street in a more subdued environment. A decent breakfast is included in the room rate.

Low-key hostel option **Blue House** (Plaza Fernández Madrid, corner of Cl. del Curato and Cra. 7 No. 38-08, tel. 5/668-6501, www.bluehouseht.com, COP$35,000 dorm, COP$150,000 d) is within the Walled City on a relatively quiet side street just a few blocks from the Plaza Santo Domingo. It's got just one dorm room and two private rooms. You'll have no problem finding the hostel—it's true blue.

OVER COP$200,000

The two classic upmarket hotels in the Walled City are the Santa Teresa and the Santa Clara. The **Hotel Charleston Santa Teresa** (Cra. 3A No.

31-23, tel. 5/664-9494, www.hotelcharlestonsan-tateresa.com, COP$718,000 d) was originally built as a convent for Clarisa nuns. Post-independence it served many different purposes: headquarters for the police, a jail, a pasta factory. In the 1980s it was finally converted into a hotel. There are two wings to this historic hotel, a colonial one and a modern wing. The two inner courtyards are lovely, and you'll be astounded by the floral displays. Concierges will help arrange any excursion you'd like. Amenities such as four restaurants, a rooftop pool, a spa, and gym ensure a relaxing stay. It's steps away from the wall.

The other old city classic is in San Diego. The Hotel Sofitel Legend Santa Clara (Cl. del Torno 39-29, tel. 5/650-4700, www.sofitel.com, COP$747,000 d) is a 122-room hotel synonymous with class and luxury. The stunning colonial courtyard alone is worth taking a peek, even if you're not a guest. The Santa Clara originally served as a convent.

From the rooftop terrace of C Hotel LM (Cl. de la Mantilla No. 3-56, tel. 5/664-9100, www.hotel-lm.com, COP$800,000 d) guests enjoy spectacular views of the rooftops of old Cartagena, including the Iglesia San Pedro Claver. This luxury hotel has seven spacious rooms and an "interactive" kitchen where guests order in advance and can even participate in food preparation.

Casa Lola (Cl. del Guerrero No. 29-108, tel. 5/664-1538, www.casalola.com.co, COP$374,000 d) is designed and managed by a Spanish couple who were some of the first hoteliers to take a chance on Getsemaní. The hotel, spread over two buildings (one colonial and one republican-era), has 10 smartly designed rooms.

It's not hard to determine how the owners decided on Makondo Hotel Boutique (Cl. del Curato No. 38-161, tel. 5/660-0823, www.hotel-makondo.com, COP$210,000 d) as the name for their small hotel: It's next door to Gabriel García Márquez's house and named for the fictitious Colombian pueblo portrayed in the author's *One Hundred Years of Solitude*. This small hotel is boutique-lite, with less exorbitant prices. It's got 10 rooms, some rather small. It's within a stone's throw of several good restaurants.

Bocagrande
OVER COP$200,000

Several mediocre hotels along Carrera 3 in Bocagrande fit in the category of economy hotels. For a little more, but for less than most hotels in Cartagena, the Hotel San Pietro (Cra. 3 No. 4-101, tel. 5/665-2369, www.pietro.com, COP$228,000 d), located on the same stretch, is more comfortable than its neighbors. It has 35 rooms of different sizes, a cute reading room with books you can check out, and a rooftop terrace with a hot tub (though it can only be used during the day, under the blazing sun). The owners also have an adjacent Italian restaurant.

The old classic in town is the Hotel Caribe (Cra. 1 No. 2-87, Bocagrande, tel. 5/650-1160, www.hotelcaribe.com, COP$350,000 d). These swanky digs, comprising three large buildings, are next to the beach (they have a beach club exclusively for guests). Most visitors, however, seem to prefer to lounge by the pools and drink a fruity cocktail.

For a no-surprises brand-name hotel experience, the Hilton Cartagena (Av. Almirante Brion, El Laguito, tel. 5/665-0660, www.hilton.com, COP$411,000 d) won't fail you. It's at the tip of Bocagrande, isolated from the crowds, and has multiple pools and restaurants as well as a gym. Guests have to pay extra for wireless Internet access, though.

FOOD

Seafood reigns supreme in Cartagena cuisine. Popular fish are *pargo rojo* (red snapper), *corvina* (sea bass), *dorado* (mahi mahi), and *sierra* (swordfish). Avoid *mero* (grouper) as it is threatened in the Caribbean waters. Shellfish include *langosta* (lobster), *langostinos* (prawns), and *chipi chipis* (tiny clams). These main dishes are often accompanied with delicious coconut rice and *patacones* (fried plantains).

Though many restaurants in the Walled City sport Manhattan prices, an inexpensive meal is not impossible to find. There are still a few mom-and-pop restaurants featuring set (cheap!) lunches for locals who would balk at paying over COP$10,000 for their midday meal.

Old City

Transport yourself to the Havana of yester-year at C La Vitrola (Cl. Baloco No. 2-01, tel. 5/664-8243, noon-3pm and 7pm-midnight daily, COP$35,000), an always elegant, always packed restaurant that specializes in Caribbean seafood, such as their popular tuna steak with avocado and mango, as well as pasta dishes. Immaculately dressed bartenders are a blur of constant motion as they perform their nightly mojito ritual: plucking mint leaves, crushing them with sugar in tall glasses, pouring in soda and rum, squeezing in some fresh lime juice, then giving the concoction a few vigorous shakes. La Vitrola is pricey, but the atmosphere, with live Cuban music in the evenings, makes it worthwhile.

Serving up the best, freshest ceviche in town is La Cevicheria (Cl. Stuart No. 7-14, tel. 5/660-1492, noon-11pm Mon.-Sat., noon-10pm Sun., COP$28,000). It's got a creative menu, featuring ceviche with mango and ceviche with coconut and lime juice, and outdoor seating on a quiet street.

Tastefully decorated with a lovely garden area, upper-crust Restaurante FM (Cl. 2 de Badillo No. 36-151, tel. 5/664-7973, noon-3pm and 7pm-11:30pm daily, COP$38,000) is named for its owner, Francisco Montoya, who has created a menu that features Caribbean and Mediterranean dishes.

El Balcón (Cl. Tumbamuertos No. 38-85, cell tel. 300/336-3876, www.elbalconcartagena.com, noon-midnight daily, COP$22,000) is a friendly place with a view in Plaza San Diego. Get here in the early evening and enjoy a sundowner cocktail as you listen to lounge music or have a light meal like a refreshing gazpacho or their shrimp "sexviche." Casual and cute, Collage Charladero (Cl. Roman No. 5-47, tel. 5/660-7626, noon-midnight Mon.-Sat., COP$22,000) serves sandwiches, burgers, falafels, fresh juices (watermelon with lime and mint), and refreshing sangria in a clean and cool environment close to all the historic sights.

The Enoteca (Cl. San Juan de Dios No. 3-39, tel. 5/664-3806, www.enoteca.com.co, noon-11:30pm daily, COP$30,000) never seems to lose its popularity. This institution is best known for its pizzas, professional service, and nice atmosphere, although its pastas are overpriced. While the interior patio decorated with fountains and twinkling lights is certainly atmospheric, you can also dine in their wine cellar room near the front, where the air conditioner always hums.

For a little curry with your shrimp, try Ganesha (Cl. de las Bovedas No. 39-91, tel. 5/660-9165, www.ganesharestaurante.com, noon-3pm and 6:30pm-11pm Tues.-Sun., COP$24,000), an authentic Indian restaurant with an extensive menu with many vegetarian options.

La Cocina de Carmela (across from Librería Nacional, Cl. Segunda de Badillo No. 36-50, cell tel. 301/348-7881, 11:30am-11pm Mon.-Sat., COP$12,000) is an unpretentious bargain spot where Colombian and international dishes (served buffet style) are on offer at lunchtime. At night it's à la carte, specializing in seafood and pasta dishes.

Crepes & Waffles (Cl. Baloco Edificio Piñeres, Local 1, tel. 5/664-6062, www.crepesywaffles.com.co, noon-10:30pm Mon.-Thurs., noon-11:30pm Fri.-Sat., 8am-10:30pm Sun.) is a wildly successful and reliable Colombian family-style chain that specializes in savory and sweet crêpes and just sweet waffles. With restaurants as far away as Spain, the restaurant has a progressive policy of hiring women who are heads of their households. Besides healthy and quick meals, Crepes is a good place for an ice cream break on a muggy Cartagena afternoon.

In 1965, Dora Gavíria starting selling her *fritos* (fried snacks) to locals and students in order to support her family of five children. Today she stays in the kitchen mostly, letting her adult children run her stand, but everyone still calls it Doña Dora (Plaza San Diego, 4pm-10pm daily). There's always a crowd gathered around the small food stall taking turns dabbing a little more hot sauce on their *arepa de huevo* (egg fried in corn meal), *carimañolas* (meat-stuffed yuca fritters), and empanadas. Beer is the perfect companion for her *fritos*. As you are strolling the narrow streets of the Old City, look for street corner vendors of *agua de coco* (coconut water). This natural sports drink is sold in the actual coconut—just add a straw. It's an unbeatable thirst quencher on hot days. The going price for coconut water is COP$2,000.

Getsemaní and Manga

The Plaza de la Trinidad in Getsemaní is the heart of the neighborhood. It's home to some swanky spots perfect for a couple of drinks or a meal. A little bit of Barcelona can be found there at the Champagnería del Mediterraneo (Plaza de la Trinidad, tel. 5/646-3576, 11am-midnight Wed.-Mon., COP$24,000), where Spanish wines accompany Serrano ham sandwiches. Demente (Plaza de la Trinidad, cell tel. 311/831-9839, www.demente.com.co, 4pm-2am Mon.-Sat., COP$22,000) is an ultra-cool tapas bar on a competing corner across the plaza that also specializes in cocktails and tapas. It's an open-air spot with a retractable roof, where the music is funky, the cocktails are fine, and the cigars are Cuban. It's a fun place for an evening of tapas and drinks.

Check out Di Silvio (Cl. de la Sierpe No. 9A-08, tel. 5/660-2205, 6:30pm-11:30pm Tues.-Sun., COP$24,000), an upscale Italian restaurant just off of the Plaza de la Trinidad. Pavia (Cl. Guerrero 29-75, tel. 5/664-3308, 6pm-midnight Mon.-Sun., COP$15,000) is a funky little pizza and pasta joint that is run by a musician and artist from Italy.

VIPs such as President Santos have been known to sample the authentic Italian dishes at I Balconi (Cl. del Guerrero No. 29-146, cell tel. 311/392-0936, www.ibalconi.com, noon-10pm Sun.-Thurs., noon-midnight Fri.-Sat., COP$18,000). It gets boisterous here as the evenings wear on and the wine flows. It's above Café Havana. Ask for a table on one of the balconies so you can enjoy the street life from on high.

At La Cocina de Pepina (Callejón Vargas, Cl. 25 No. 9A-06, Local 2, tel. 5/664-2944,

noon-4pm and 6pm-10pm Tues.-Sat., noon-4pm Sun.-Mon., COP$25,000), typical dishes from across the Caribbean coast are thoughtfully reinvented. It's a cozy place in an alleyway near the Calle del Arsenal. Make a reservation for dinner.

Marea by Rausch (Centro de Convenciones, Cra. 8, tel. 5/654-4205, www.mareabyrausch.com, noon-3pm and 7pm-10pm Tues.-Sat., 4pm-10pm Sun., COP$45,000) is an ultra-chic seafood restaurant that is the brainchild of the Rausches, two brother chefs from Bogotá. Specialties include a tuna tartar and prawns in a coconut and saffron sauce. This restaurant has excellent views of the bay and the Torre del Reloj.

The food at the Club de Pesca (Fuerte San Sebastián del Pastelilo, Manga, tel. 5/660-4594, noon-11pm daily, COP$55,000) is overpriced and overrated, but the view is unsurpassable. This Cartagena classic is in the old San Sebastián del Pastelillo fort with magnificent views to the bay. It's a favorite spot for wedding banquets, and some guests arrive at the fort in yachts. On the menu try the *jaiba gratinada,* which is a crab au gratin.

Bocagrande

Elegant Arabe Internacional (Cra. 3 No. 8-83, tel. 5/665-4365, www.restaurantearabeinternacional.com, noon-3:30pm and 7pm-10pm Mon.-Fri., noon-10pm Sat.-Sun., COP$25,000) has been serving authentic Middle Eastern cuisine since 1965. It's a popular place for the Cartagena business crowd.

If you just want a hearty, authentic Colombian meal without the bells and whistles, head to Mac Dugan's (Av. San Martín No. 9-42, tel. 5/665-5101, 11am-9pm daily, COP$12,000), a family-run restaurant in Bocagrande.

INFORMATION AND SERVICES

In addition to locations at the airport and at the cruise ship port, there are city-run tourist information kiosks near the Torre del Reloj (no phone,

9am-noon and 1pm-6pm Mon.-Sat., 9am-5pm Sun.) and an air-conditioned main office in the historic Casa de Marquez Plaza de la Aduana (tel. 5/660-1583, 9am-noon and 1pm-6pm Mon.-Sat., 9am-5pm Sun.). The website for the Cartagena Tourism Board is www.cartagenadeindias.travel.

In case of an emergency, call the police at 123, 112, or 5/628-4748. For medical emergencies call tel. 5/667-5244.

Although postcards are relatively easy to purchase, sending them is a different matter. Mailing postcards and letters is not common here and not that easy. The post office, 4-72, has a branch in the Walled City (Cl. de la Moneda No. 7-94, tel. 5/670-0102, 8am-noon and 2pm-5:30pm Mon.-Fri., 9am-12:30pm Sat.). It costs COP$2,000 for postage to the United States and Canada. This branch has a small exhibition space with old postage stamps on display.

Volunteering

The Fundación Juan Felipe Gómez (Cl. 31 No. 91-80, Ternera, tel. 5/661-0937, www.juanfe. org) was the inspiration of Catalina Escobar, a Colombian businesswoman. As a volunteer in a maternity clinic in Cartagena, she was holding a tiny infant, born to a teenage mother, who died in her arms, all because the mother didn't have the most basic financial resources to get proper care for her son. Within days, Escobar's own son died in a tragic death. Driven by grief and the desire to help young women to lead healthy and happy lives, she founded this organization. At the Fundación Juan Felipe Gómez, named for the child she lost, young women (often pregnant or new mothers) take classes designed to provide them with workforce skills. Because of Escobar's efforts, she was nominated a CNN Hero of the Year in 2012. Anybody with skill or interest in nutrition, computers, fashion, or teaching English can get involved. Both short- and long-term volunteers are welcomed. If you'd like to visit the center, call in advance to arrange a tour. You can take a public bus or a 20-minute taxi to the *fundación*.

GETTING THERE

Cartagena's Aeropuerto Internacional Rafael Núñez (CTG, tel. 5/656-9202, www.sacsa.com.co) is located to the east of the city, about a 12-minute cab ride from Cartagena.

JetBlue (www.jetblue.com) operates three flights a week between New York-JFK and Cartagena. Nonstop from Florida, Spirit Airlines (www.spirit.com) has a flight from Fort Lauderdale, and Avianca (Col. toll-free tel. 01/800-095-3434, www.avianca.com) has one out of Miami. Copa (tel. 5/665-8495, www. copaair.com) serves Cartagena from its hub in Panama City, Panama. The main national carriers, Avianca and LAN Colombia (Col. toll-free tel. 01/800-094-9490, www.lan.com), operate many flights each day to Cartagena from various Colombian cities. Viva Colombia (tel. 5/642-4989, www.vivacolombia.co) often offers inexpensive fares between Cartagena and Medellín, Bogotá, Cali, and Pereira. ADA (Col. toll-free tel. 01/800-051-4232, www.ada-aero.com) serves the city with flights from Medellín, Montería, and Cúcuta. Easy Fly (tel. 5/693-0400, www.easyfly.co) has a nonstop from Bucaramanga.

Regular bus service connects Cartagena with all major cities and all coastal cities. The Terminal de Transportes (Diag. 56N. 57-236, tel. 5/663-0454) is a long 20- to 30-minute cab ride from the *centro histórico*. Expect to pay about COP$20,000 for the trip.

GETTING AROUND

The Old City, Getsemaní, and Bocagrande are very walkable. For short hops, there are cabs. Taxis here do not have meters, so it's quite possible you won't get the local rate. Before hopping in a cab, ask a local or two how much you should pay. From the Old City to Bocagrande, expect to pay around COP$6,000. A ride to the airport will cost COP$10,000, and a trip to Las Américas will go for COP$12,000. Tipping is not customary for cabbies. Although an additional cost is added if you use a phone service for a cab, added costs for night pickups, air conditioning, and traveling on holidays are not permitted, and you can protest those.

It may seem overwhelming at first, but taking a public bus is a cheap way to get from point A to point B—and you'll hardly ever be overcharged. To hop on a bus to Bocagrande from the Old City, walk down to Avenida Santander along the sea and flag down just about any bus you see (or look for a sign in the window that reads "Bocagrande"). The ride will set you back COP$1,500. When you want out, yell "¡Parada!" On the main road just to the east of the walls, you'll see a nonstop parade of buses loading and unloading. From here you can go to the Castillo de San Felipe, to the Mercado de Bazurto, or to the bus terminal, for the same low price of COP$1,500.

BOCACHICA

Bocachica, which means "Small Mouth," is one of two entrances to the Bahía de Cartagena. It is at the southern end of the bay. The other, much wider entrance, is Bocagrande ("Big Mouth"), in the northern part of the bay near Cartagena. In 1640, when three galleons sank at Bocagrande and blocked that passage, the Spaniards decided to fortify the more easily defensible Bocachica.

The Fuerte de San Fernando and Batería de San José are two forts constructed at either side of Bocachica that were the first line of defense of the bay. The Fuerte de San Fernando, at the southern tip of the island of Tierrabomba, is a particularly impressive example of 18th-century military architecture. It is very well preserved and you can still see the barracks, kitchen, storerooms, and chapel enclosed within the massive fortifications. The low-lying Batería de San José is a much more modest affair. The only way to get to Bocachica is by lanchas that depart from the Muelle de los Pegasos, the tourist port in Cartagena near the Torre del Reloj (COP$7,000). The 45-minute trip through the bay provides interesting views of Cartagena and the port. In Bocachica, there are a few small restaurants where you can eat fried fish, coconut rice, and patacones (fried plantains) and drink a cold beer.

PLAYA BLANCA AND ISLAS DEL ROSARIO

South of Cartagena is the elongated island of Barú, which is separated from the mainland by the Canal del Dique, a manmade waterway built in 1650 to connect Cartagena with the Río Magdalena. On Barú lies Playa Blanca, a Caribbean paradise of idyllic, white-sand beaches bordering warm waters of dozens of shades of blue. West of Barú, and about 25 kilometers southwest of Cartagena, is the archipelago Islas del Rosario, part of the much larger Parque Nacional Natural Corales del Rosario y San Bernardo. On Barú and the Islas del Rosario, traditional Afro-Colombian communities with rich cultural heritages coexist with the vacation houses of Colombia's rich and famous.

Barú is home to several beautiful beaches. With the exception of Playa Blanca, most of these are inaccessible to the general public. The 25 small coral islands of the Islas del Rosario are a marine wonderland. The once-spectacular coral reefs off of Barú and surrounding the archipelago have been badly damaged by the increased flow of fresh water from the Canal del Dique, which has been dredged in recent years.

A trip to Playa Blanca and the Islas del Rosario affords the chance to blissfully bask in the sun and splash about in the ocean. However, be aware that the standard tours, such as those operated by Optitours (Av. Santander No. 46-94, Cartagena, tel. 5/666-5957, cell tel. 300/394-4848, www.opitours.com, COP$50,000-70,000) can often be crowded on weekends. Most tours involve cruising down the Bahía de Cartagena, passing through the Strait of Bocachica, and heading to the Oceanario Islas del Rosario (www.oceanariocolombia.com, 10am-3pm Tues.-Sun., COP$25,000) on the island of San Martín de Pajarales, part of the Islas del Rosario. Very popular with Colombian families on vacation, the aquarium features a dolphin show. You can swim in the water and rest in the shade if you decide not to patronize the aquarium. Then the boats head off to Playa Blanca, where you can buy lunch. The insistent vendors at Playa Blanca can make for an unpleasant experience, but you can try telling them *"no, gracias."*

If you are willing to pay more, there are more upscale day tours to the *islas*. One is a day trip (COP$173,000) to the luxurious beachside Hotel San Pedro de Majagua (Cartagena office: Cl. del Torno No. 39-29, tel. 5/650-4460, http:// nuevo.hotelmajagua.com, COP$400,000 d) on Isla Grande. They take care of transportation from the Muelle de Marina Santa Cruz in Manga (boats leave at 9am daily). The price also includes a seafood lunch and a visit to the Oceanario Islas del Rosario, whether you want to go there or not. You can also spend the night at this comfortable hotel (COP$350,000 d including transportation).

Another recommended day tour is the This Is Cartagena (Av. Centenario No. 30-42, tel. 5/660-0969, cell tel. 317/259-3773, www.thisis-cartagena.com, 9am-6pm Mon.-Fri., yacht tour COP$200,000) tour to the islands. It's a more relaxed experience, as groups are rarely larger than eight persons.

If you are willing to splurge on an overnight stay, upscale hotel options include Coralina Isla Boutique (cell tel. 310/764-8835, COP$577,000 d) or Agua Azul Beach Resort (cell tel. 320/680-2134 or 314/504-3540, COP$1,300,000 d high season, COP$700,000 d low season). For a special occasion, you can rent the luxurious houseboat run by the travel agency Aviatur. Their Casa Navegante (tel. 1/587-5181, www.aviaturecoturismo.com, COP$1,200,000) is moored on the beautiful Bahía Cholón in the Islas de Rosario.

MOMPOX

This town, founded in 1540 on the eastern edge of a large island between two branches of the Río Magdalena (the Brazo de Loba and the Brazo Mompox), was an opulent center of trade, connecting the interior of the country with Cartagena during the colonial era. But then the mighty river changed its course in the late 18th century. Mompox's importance steadily declined, never to return.

Mompox is what Cartagena looked like before it became a tourist destination, and it's hard to deny

© ANDREW DIER

The Río Magdalena runs through Mompox.

the melancholic charm this oppressively hot town retains even today. The attraction here is strolling the wide streets, admiring the magnificent whitewashed houses decorated with intricate iron latticework, and watching the river flow by. In 1995, because of its architectural importance, it was declared a UNESCO World Heritage Site.

The town is spread out along the river. It does not have a central plaza, but three squares, each with a church, facing the river. It is believed that each of these squares is on the location of a former indigenous settlement. From south to north these are: Plaza de Santa Bárbara, Plaza de la Concepción (also known as Plaza Mayor), and Plaza de San Francisco. Three main streets run parallel to the river: Calle de la Albarrada (which corresponds to Carrera 1) facing the river; the Calle Real del Medio, Mompox's main street, one block west of the river; and the Calle de Atrás (literally, the "street behind").

There are two historical churches worth visiting in Mompox. However, they are only regularly open during mass times. Nonetheless, the Casa Amarilla can call the church to request that someone open up the doors so that you can take a quick peek. The Iglesia de Santa Bárbara (Cl. de la Albarrada and Cl. 14, mass 4pm Sun.), built in 1630, is well worth a visit. The facade is painted a striking yellow, with colorful floral decorations. It has an unusual baroque octagonal tower with a balcony wrapping around it. Inside, it has a magnificent gilded altar. Another noteworthy church is the Iglesia de San Agustín (Cl. Real del Medio and Cl. 17, masses 7pm daily, with additional 9am mass on Sun.), which houses the Santo Sepulcro, a gilded reproduction of Christ's tomb, which is carried through the streets during Semana Santa. The only museum in town is the Museo Cultural de Arte Religioso (Cl. Real del Medio No. 17-07, tel. 5/685-6074, 9am-noon and 3pm-4pm Tues. and Thurs.-Fri., 9am-noon Sat.-Mon., COP$2,000), which has displays of gold- and silverwork from the colonial era. Mompox silver- and goldsmiths made a name for themselves with their intricate filigree jewelry. Another interesting sight is the Piedra de

the ornate Iglesia de Santa Bárbara, Mompóx

© ANDREW DIER

Bolívar (Cl. de la Albarrada and Cl. 17), a monument facing the river with a stone slab that lists all the visits Simón Bolívar made to Mompox. Finally, Mompox's atmospheric 19th-century Cementerio Municipal (Cl. 18 and Cra. 4, 8am-noon and 2-5pm daily, free) is well worth a detour.

Festivals and Events

Semana Santa, or Holy Week (Easter), which is held during late March or April, is the most important celebration in Mompox, when visitors from all over Colombia converge on the town to watch its religious processions and attend concerts. You'll have to book months in advance to get a hotel room during that time.

Shopping

Mompox is famous for its intricate gold filigree jewelry. Look for the Joyería Filimompox (Cl. 23 No. 3-23, tel. 5/685-6604 or 313/548-2322), where the staff will explain their craft to you during your visit to their workshop. They accept credit cards. At the Escuela Taller de Artes y Oficios de Santa Cruz de Mompox (Claustro de San Agustín, Cl. 16 No. 1A-57, tel. 5/685-5204), young people learn traditional handicrafts. Visitors are welcome to drop by and watch these artisans at work. Inside, there's an interior courtyard, an inviting place to linger for a while.

Accommodations and Food

Bioma Hotel Boutique (Cl. Real del Medio No. 18-59, tel. 5/685-6733, cell tel. 315/308-6365, www.bioma.co, COP$190,000 d) may be one of the most comfortable options in town, as it offers 12 air-conditioned rooms, a dipping pool, and good food. The ⓒ Casa Amarilla (Cl. de la Albarrada No. 13-59, tel. 5/685-6326, cell tel. 301/362-7065, www.lacasaamaraillamompos.com, COP$25,000 dorm, COP$100,000 d), owned by a British travel writer, is another excellent choice, with accommodations for the backpacker as well as private rooms for those seeking more comfort. After a careful restoration, the Casa Amarilla opened a luxury colonial house called the Casa de la Concepción (Cl. de la Albarrada No. 13-59, tel. 5/685-6326, cell tel. 301/362-7065, www.lacasaamaraillamompos. com, COP$1,500,000 house rental) in 2013. It has four bedrooms and two interior patio gardens, and the second story balcony has a fine view to the plaza below.

Hotels in Mompox are the best options food-wise, but be sure to confirm with them before arriving. During off-season many do not have cooks on call. Otherwise, the Comedor Costeño (Cl. de la Albarrada No. 18-45, tel. 5/685-5263, 7am-5pm daily) is a restaurant that serves *comida típica* (Colombian fare) overlooking the Magdalena. On the renovated Plaza de la Concepción there are some open-air cafés that serve snacks and drinks. This is a nice weekend night gathering area. Plaza Santo Domingo (Cl. 18 and Cra. 3) has food stalls serving pizza and other fast food.

Getting There

Most visitors arrive in Mompox from Cartagena, and there are several ways to make the journey.

There is one direct bus that leaves from the Terminal de Transportes in Cartagena (Diagonal 57 No. 24-236, tel. 5/663-0454) at 6:30am. The ride takes eight hours and costs COP$50,000. More comfortable is a door-to-door service (COP$75,000) with a company like Toto Express (cell tel. 310/707-0838), which takes six hours. The fastest way involves a van, a boat, and a taxi: take a van (COP$40,000 pp, 3.5 hours) from outside the Terminal de Transportes in Cartagena to Magangué, a port on the Magdalena; there hop on a *chalupa* boat that will take you to a spot called Bodega de Mompox (COP$7,000, 30 mins.); and from there take a shared taxi or *mototaxi* (COP$15,000, 30 minutes) to Mompox.

Barranquilla

Colombia's fourth largest city (pop. 1.6 million) is known for its busy port and for the bacchanalian Carnaval de Barranquilla, designated a World Masterpiece of the Oral and Intangible Heritage of Humanity by UNESCO. This, the most famous celebration in Colombia, is a time of music, dancing in the streets, and revelry. It lasts only about four days, but the city starts readying for it days (if not weeks) in advance.

During the rest of the year there's not a whole lot to lure the visitor to Barranquilla. It is not a colonial city, but vestiges of its early 20th century importance can be seen in its El Prado district.

SIGHTS

Two museums give the visitor a good insight into Barranquilla's people and culture. The first, Casa del Carnaval (Cra. 54 No. 49B-39, tel. 5/370-5437 or 5/379-6621, 9am-5pm Tues.-Thurs., 9am-6pm Sat.-Sun., COP$5,000), is *carnaval* headquarters,

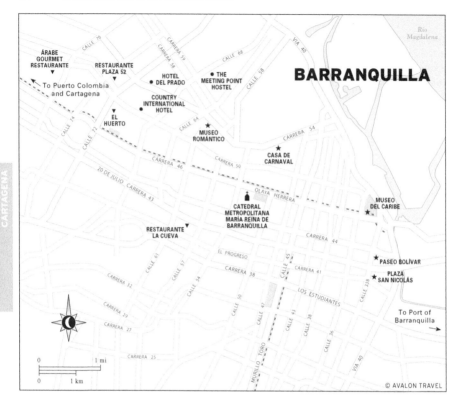

and its Sala Carnaval Elsa Caridi provides an inter-active introduction to the annual event. After a visit here, you'll come to understand the many different components of the celebration, like the different musical styles: *cumbia, mapalé, chandé,* and *son.* While at first blush it may seem that the Carnaval de Baranquilla is just a big party, there is more to it than meets the eye. Behind every costume, parade, and dance there is a story. Knowledgeable guides will share this story and their genuine enthusiasm for the festival at this well-done museum.

The second of Barranquilla's top two museums is Museo del Caribe (Cl. 36 No. 46-66, tel. 5/372-0582, www.culturacaribe.org, 8am-5pm Tues.-Fri., 9am-6pm Sat.-Sun., COP$10,000), one of the finest museums in the country, with a focus on Costeño (Caribbean coast) culture. There is a room

dedicated to Gabriel García Márquez, which may be hard to understand if you are not familiar with many of his works or if your Spanish isn't perfect; slide shows on ecosystems from the Caribbean region; and exhibits on the people of the Caribbean, including the many different indigenous tribes who live there. Of particular interest is a room that examines immigration to the region, from African slaves to "Turcos," meaning those mostly coming from Syria, Lebanon, and Palestine. The museum has a restaurant with reasonably priced meals and a cute, tiny café on the plaza in front. Both of these keep regular museum hours.

The old downtown of the city is very real, in its rundown and dirty state. The Paseo Bolívar (Cl. 34 between Cras. 38-45) is the main drag downtown. It's lined with discount shops and charming used-book stands, where you can often find some Colombian classics—even in English—if you look hard enough. There's always a crowd at the newspaper kiosks, which seems like a scene from a different era. On the restored Plaza San Nicolás (between Clls. 32-33 and Cras. 41-42) is the neogothic Iglesia San Nicolás Tolentino (Cra. 42 No. 33-45, tel. 5/340-2247), which took about 300 years to build.

Not about roses and chocolates, the Museo Romántico (Cra. 54 No. 59-199, tel. 5/344-4591, 9am-11:30am and 2:30pm-5:30pm Mon.-Fri., COP$5,000) is really a history museum of Barranquilla with artwork, old *carnaval* costumes, missives signed by Simón Bolívar, and a typewriter used by Gabriel García Márquez. It was once the majestic home of Jewish immigrants who arrived in Colombia at the turn of the 20th century. It is run by an elderly historian and his wife.

Pop singer Shakira has won two Grammys and countless other awards, and is Barranquilla's favorite daughter. To honor her, the people of the city put a statue of her stroking a guitar in a prominent place: in front of the Estadio Metropolitano Roberto Meléndez (Aves. Circunvalar Alberto Pumarejo and Murillo).

FESTIVALS AND EVENTS
◖ Carnaval de Barranquilla

For most Colombians, Barranquilla is synonymous with *carnaval*, and they boast that the Carnaval de Barranquilla is the world's biggest after Rio, although folks from New Orleans may balk at this claim. In Colombia, this is really the only place where the bacchanal is celebrated, although some Caribbean cities and even Bogotá make an effort.

During the four days prior to Ash Wednesday, in late February or early March, the Carnaval de Barranquilla (www.carnavaldebarranquilla.org) is full of Costeño pageantry: costumes, music, dance, parades, and whiskey.

Officially, Carnaval gets going on Saturday, but on the Friday night before, La Guacherna is held. One event of the night is the Desfile Gay, which is when outrageously costumed men dressed in drag

parade down a street to the hoots and hollers of thousands of bystanders.

Saturday is the main event. That's the day of the Batalla de las Flores (Battle of the Flowers) parade. It's when floats carrying beauty queens and dancers and thousands in *comparsas* (groups) in elaborate costumes make their way down the Calle 40 under the sizzling Barranquilla sun. This event dates back to 1903, when the celebration was begun as a celebration of the end of the Guerra de Mil Días (Thousand Days' War). Participation in the parades is serious business here, involving planning, practice, money, and, sometimes, connections. However, there is one *comparsa* during the Batalla de las Flores in which just about anyone can participate, and it's one of the most popular. That's the *comparsa* of "Disfrazate como Quieras"—go however you like. Anybody in a costume, from the silly to the sexy, can join. To participate, visit the web page (www.disfrazatecomoquieras.com).

On Sunday, during the Gran Parada de Tradición y Folclor, groups of dancers perform on the Calle 40 to the typical, hypnotic music of *carnaval*—a mix of African, indigenous, and European sounds. On Monday there is another parade, the Gran Parade de Comparsas, and, starting in the late afternoon, a massive concert attracting more than 30 musical groups. These compete for the award of Congo del Oro. On Tuesday, after four days of music and dancing, things wind down with the parade Joselito Se Va con las Cenizas. This is when Joselito, a fictitious Barranquillero, dies after four days of rumba, and his body is carried through the streets as bystanders weep. On Wednesday, Barranquilleros call in sick.

You can watch all the action of the parades from the *palcos* (bleachers) that line Calle 40. Keep in mind that the parades take place in the middle of the day, meaning lots of sun and heat. Tickets for the *palcos* can be ordered online at Tu Boleta (www.tuboleta.com).

With regard to *carnaval*, it's said that "*quien lo vive, es quien lo goza*" ("whoever experiences it is who enjoys it"). But to do that, it's crucial to get those hotel and flight reservations early.

ACCOMMODATIONS

As a business destination, Barranquilla has a number of hotel options, although hostels are almost nonexistent. Rates significantly drop on weekends. **Meeting Point Hostel** (Cra. 61 No. 68-100, tel. 5/318-2599, www.themeetingpoint.hostel. com, COP$60,000 d, COP$25,000 dorm) is the only hostel catering to international backpackers in Barranquilla. It's run by an Italian-Colombian family. If it feels like you're staying in their house, that's because it is their house, down to kids on the sofa playing video games. The neighborhood is quiet and green, and about a 15-minute walk from the El Prado area.

Country International Hotel (Cra. 52 No. 75-30, tel. 5/369-5900, ext. 120, www.countryinthotel. com, COP$238,000 d) has a nice pool and comfortable rooms. It's located in a good area. **Hotel Estelar Alto Prado** (Cl. 76 No. 56-29, tel. 5/336-0000, COP$292,000 d) is a modern, ultra comfortable, and stylish address in Barranquilla.

C Hotel El Prado (Cra. 54 No. 70-10, tel. 5/369-7777, www.hotelelpradosa.com, COP$236,000 d) debuted in 1930, and for decades, before the relatively recent boom in luxury cookie-cutter hotels, it was the luxury address in town. It's got 200 rooms, a massive boiler room, and a fab pool to lounge around drinking a cocktail. Nonguests can spend an afternoon getting pampered here for only COP$38,000, a price that includes lunch and all the poolside lounging you need.

FOOD

El Huerto (Cra. 52 No. 70-139, tel. 5/368-7171, 8am-7:30pm Mon.-Sat., 10am-3pm Sun., COP$12,000) has been serving the vegetarian minority of Barranquilla since 1986. They have a set lunch menu every day and sell baked goods to go as well.

Barranquilla's many residents of Lebanese and Syrian descent have a few Middle Eastern restaurants to choose from. One of the best is **Arabe Gourmet** (Cra. 49C No. 76-181, tel. 5/360-5930, 11am-10pm daily, COP$25,000).

The **C Restaurante Bar La Cueva** (Cra. 43 No. 59-03, tel. 5/340-9813, noon-3pm and 6pm-10pm Mon.-Thurs., noon-3pm and 6pm-1am Fri.-Sat., COP$25,000) has history and lots of character. It was the hangout of Gabriel García Márquez and artists such as Alejandro Obregón in the 1960s. Elephant tracks, memorabilia, and photos make it seem like a museum, but it is still a restaurant, and a popular one at that. The specialty here is seafood. There's live music on Friday and Saturday evenings. Be sure to check out the Obregón work *La Mulata de Obregón,* complete with a bullet hole thanks to a drunken friend of the artist.

For steak lovers, the top two options in Barranquilla are **La Bonga del Sinu** (Cra. 53 No. 82-10, tel. 5/358-5035, 11:30am-10pm Mon.-Wed., 11:30am-11pm Thurs.-Sat., 11:30am-9pm Sun., COP$25,000) and **Buffalo Grill** (Cra. 51B No. 79-97, Local 2, tel. 5/378-6519, noon-11pm Mon.-Thurs., noon-midnight Fri.-Sat., noon-10pm Sun., COP$25,000).

Thanks to its location in a strip mall, you may not have soaring expectations for **Restaurante Plaza 52** (Cra. 52 No. 72-114, Local C9, tel. 5/358-1806, 10am-8pm daily, COP$6,500 set lunch). But the lunchtime crowds (and lines) give it away. They serve great down-home food at rock-bottom prices.

Barranquilla's version of street food can be found at the popular, competing **food stands** at the intersection of Carrera 52 and Calle 71. There's always a crowd composed of construction workers and office types hanging out here.

GETTING THERE

From Barranquilla's **Aeropuerto Internacional Ernesto Cortissoz** (Soledad, www.baq.aero), there is excellent air connection with all major cities in Colombia and a handful of nonstop international flights as well. The airport is south of the city in Soledad. Taxis cost about COP$20,000 from downtown to the airport.

Avianca (Centro Comercial Gran Centro Cra. 53 No. 68-242, tel. 5/360-7007, www.avianca.com, 8am-noon and 2pm-6pm Mon.-Fri., 9am-12:30pm Sat.) flies nonstop from Miami, Bogotá, Cali, and Medellín. **LAN** (Centro Comercial Buenavista Cra.

53 No. 98-99, Col. toll-free tel. 01/800-094-9490, 10am-8pm Mon.-Fri., 10am-noon and 1pm-7pm Sat., 10am-noon and 1pm-5pm Sun.) has flights to Bogotá. On Copa (Col. toll-free tel. 01/800-011-2600, www.copair.com) there are nonstop flights to San Andrés and to Panama City.

Viva Colombia (tel. 5/319-7989, www.viva-colombia.com.co) flies from Medellín, Easy Fly (tel. 5/385-0676, www.easyfly.com.co) has nonstop flights from Bucaramanga and Valledupar, and ADA (Col. toll-free tel. 01/800-051-4232, www.ada-aero.com) flies from Montería.

There is regular bus service to all points in Colombia from the Terminal Metropolitana de Transportes (Km. 1.5 Prolongación Cl. Murillo, tel. 5/323-0034, www.ttbag.com.co). Fast van service is also available to Cartagena (COP$17,000) and Santa Marta (COP$17,000) from the Berlinastur terminal in town (Cl. 96 No. 46-36, tel. 5/385-0030, www.berlinastur.com).

GETTING AROUND

Barranquilla is not much of a walking city, with taxi cabs the most convenient way to get around. Unfortunately the cabs are not metered, so you might be charged a little more than locals if you're unfamiliar with rates. In town, you should never pay more than COP$13,000 to get from point A to point B. For those with smartphones, the app Tappsi enables you to order a cab from anywhere in the city, receive the license plate number and name of the driver, and send this information to a friend, for security purposes.

Transmetro (www.transmetro.gov.co, 5am-11pm Mon.-Sat., 6am-10pm Sun., COP$1,400) is the Barranquilla version of the TransMilenio rapid bus system in Bogotá, and it runs along two main avenues: Avenida Murillo (also known as Calle 45) and Avenida Olaya Herrera (also known as Carrera 46). There are stations in front of the Museo del Caribe, the cathedral, and the stadium, and you can take the bus downtown from there.

PUERTO COLOMBIA

About a 40-minute bus ride (COP$2,000) outside of Barranquilla is Puerto Colombia, which was once Colombia's most important port.

The pier, the main attraction in town, was built at the turn of the 20th century. At the time, it was one of the longest piers in the world. The pier was severely damaged in major storms in 2009 and 2013, and there are huge gaps in the pier today. Today you can walk the pier and ask local fishers about their catch. Military personnel stand guard, meanwhile, in order to prohibit smuggling of illegal contraband. There are plans to refurbish the pier and to create an artificial beach, in hope of attracting weekend day-trippers and bringing back some of the town's former glory. Part of that effort included the construction of a boardwalk along the water.

The old train station has been converted into a cultural center by the Fundación Puerto Colombia (town center, tel. 5/309-6120, fundacionpuertocoombia@gmail.com, 8:30am-12:30pm and 3pm-7pm Mon.-Fri., 9am-1pm Sat., 4pm-6pm Sun., free), and there is often an art exhibit going on here.

There are several seafood restaurants around the pier area. The most famous, perhaps, is Mi Viejo Muelle (Cl. 2 No. 3-175, tel. 5/309-6727, noon-8pm daily, COP$22,000). It's got a nice large deck with a view, and old photos of Puerto Colombia decorate the walls.

CARTAGENA

Santa Marta

Santa Marta is coming into its own as a major tourist destination on the Caribbean coast. In addition to its charming historic district, great hotel options, and restaurants, Santa Marta offers an excellent base from which to explore the Sierra Nevada and the deserts of La Guajira.

Santa Marta was the first permanent Spanish settlement in colonial Colombia, and remained relatively rural until the second half of the 20th century, when it became a major domestic tourist destination. In the mid-1970s, treasure hunters discovered Ciudad Perdida high in the Sierra. Ciudad Perdida was one of the most important settlements of the Tayrona indigenous people. The National Institute of Anthropology carefully excavated the site, opening it to tourism in the 1980s.

In recent years, the old historic downtown, long neglected as development had moved to the Rodadero district, has seen a renaissance. It has become a destination of its own and a staging point for visits to the unspoiled beaches of Parque Nacional Natural Tayrona and hiking trips to Ciudad Perdida.

ORIENTATION

The *centro histórico* extends from the busy Calle 22 (Avenida Santa Rita) in the west to the Avenida del Ferrocarril in the east, toward the seaside village of Taganga. And from south to north, the borders are

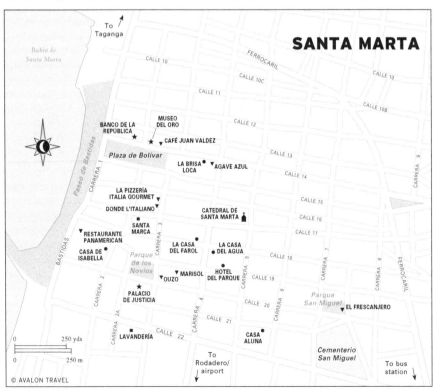

SANTA MARTA

the same Avenida del Ferrocarril in the south to the *malecón* (Carrera 1C/Avenida Rodrigo de Bastidas). The focal point of the Centro is the Parque de los Novios (Carreras 2A-3 and Calles 19-20). This is a lovely park with pedestrian streets (Calle 19 and Carrera 3) intersecting on its eastern side. Most sights are within a smaller range of streets from Carrera 5 (Camp Serrano) to the water and between Calles 20 and 14.

The Rodadero district is a mini-Miami with condos and hotels lining the beach. It's west of downtown Santa Marta, just around the bend on the main highway. There are constant bus links all day between the two.

SIGHTS
Centro Histórico

The compact *centro histórico* in Santa Marta in itself feels like a living museum, with its mix of colonial and republican-era architecture. All major sights, save for the Quinta de San Pedro Alejandrino, are located here and can be visited in one day.

The Parque de los Novios (Cras. 2A-3 and Clls. 19-20) is a symbol of the city's rejuvenation. The pedestrian streets (except for one) around the plaza have a lot to do with it. Today it's a most pleasant place for a stroll and a meal. Restaurants have cropped up along the park's periphery. On the Calle 20 side of the park is the grandiose neoclassical Palacio de Justicia. Visitors can only admire it from the outside, as the building is not open to the public.

The Catedral de Santa Marta or Basílica Menor (Cr. 5 No. 16-30, tel. 5/421-2434, masses at noon and 6pm Mon.-Sat., 7am, 10am, noon, and 6pm Sun.) took around 30 years to build and was completed in 1794, toward the end of Spanish reign in Nueva Granada, as colonial Colombia was called. It is one of the oldest cathedrals in Latin America. The city's founder, Rodrigo de Bastidas, is buried there, and Simón Bolívar laid in rest there before his body was moved to Caracas.

The Plaza de Bolívar (Cras. 1-2 and Clls. 14-15) has a statue of Simón Bolívar on horseback, ready to destroy the oppressors. The Banco de la República

(Cl. 14 No. 1C-37, tel. 5/421-0251, www.banrep.gov.co, 8:30am-6pm Mon.-Fri., 9am-1pm Sat., free) often has art exhibits and also has a public library on the third floor (a quiet place to read or work).

The Museo de Oro Tairona (Cl. 14 No. 1C-37, tel. 5/421-0251, www.banrepcultural.org, 8:30am-6pm Mon.-Fri., 9am-1pm Sat., free) is in the historic Casa de la Aduana, perhaps the oldest customs house in the Americas, dating back to 1531. A smaller version of the famous Museo del Oro in Bogotá, this focuses on the Tayrona people, who were the native settlers of the region and forebears of the Kogis, Arhuacos, Kankuamos, and Wiwas who live in the Sierra Nevada. There are ceramic and gold artifacts on display, and a description of the Ciudad Perdida archaeological site. A visit to this museum may enrich your hike up to the Lost City, as you'll have a better understanding of the people who once inhabited it.

Along the waterfront is the Paseo de Bastidas (Cra. 1) boardwalk. A sunset walk along the pier that extends from the boardwalk is a daily Santa Marta ritual. Great views are to be had here of the port on the right, the Isla Morro in the sea, and the gorgeous sailboats on the left docked at the Marina Santa Marta.

Quinta de San Pedro Alejandrino

The Liberator, Simón Bolívar, spent his final days in Santa Marta, passing away at the age of 47 at the Quinta de San Pedro Alejandrino (Mamatoco, tel. 5/433-2995, www.museobolivariano.org.co, 9am-6pm daily, COP$12,000). This country estate is now a museum where visitors can see the bedroom in which Bolívar died in 1830. A modern wing houses two art galleries. Young guides will offer to take you around the complex for a small tip of about COP$2,000, but you're probably better off on your own. The *quinta* is set in a manicured botanical garden. There is a small snack bar and gift shop on the grounds.

SHOPPING

The shop Santa Marca (Cl. 17 No. 2-45, tel. 5/423-5862, www.santamarca.co, 8am-8pm Mon.-Sat.)

Locals converge on Santa Marta's Paseo de Bastidas to enjoy the sunset.

© ANDREW DIER

has gifts and souvenirs made by local creative types. The **Centro Comercial Arrecife** (Cra. 4 No. 11A-119, tel. 5/422-8873, 9am-9pm daily) is a large shopping mall in the Rodadero area; it has a food court, a Carulla supermarket, a movie theater, and a selection of mostly Colombian brand clothing shops.

RECREATION

Deva Yoga Studio (Cra. 21 No. 15-18, tel. 5/431-0354, www.newfuturesociety.org, classes at 9am and 6:30pm Mon.-Fri., 9am Sat., COP$20,000/class) offers hatha and Tibetan yoga classes and meditation classes. It is affiliated with the New Future Society International, an international yoga organization.

The tour agency **Aventura Sierra Nevada** (Restaurante Marisol, Cra. 3A No. 16-30, cell tel. 311/216-5419, www.aventurasierranevada.com, 10am-9pm daily) organizes activities along the Caribbean coast, from kite surfing courses to bike tours of various lengths, hikes to Tayronaka, a trip to the Yumake nature reserve, and inner tube trips down the Río Don Diego.

ACCOMMODATIONS

The Centro Histórico of Santa Marta was considered to be crumbling, desolate, and even dangerous before the early 2000s, but gentrification has taken hold and today it's gone boutique. In addition to posh boutique hotels, there are comfortable hostels. The Rodadero has plenty of high-rise hotels, most of which are all-inclusive. The village of Taganga is also very close to the city, and some prefer to stay at this relaxed beach village and visit Santa Marta for the day or head to restaurants in the Centro Histórico in the evenings.

Under COP$70,000

Aluna (Cl. 21 No. 5-27, tel. 5/432-4916, www.alunahotel.com, COP$30,000 dorm with fan, COP$100,000 d with a/c) gets just about everything right. This hostel has a mix of dorm rooms and private rooms, all immaculate, each with private bath. There's plenty of space to hang out over the three floors of the hostel. There is a small shaded interior courtyard and an excellent

The Quinta de San Pedro Alejandrino is where Simón Bolívar spent his final days.

top floor terrace that provides vantage points over the city and to the Sierra Nevada in the distance. The hostel restaurant serves gazpacho, falafel, and, for breakfast, those banana pancakes that every traveler craves. It's run by a friendly Dubliner, Patrick.

Fun and high energy: That's La Brisa Loca (Cl. 14 No. 3-58, tel. 5/431-6121, www.labrisaloca.com, COP$28,000 dorm, COP$90,000 d), a revamped mansion turned hostel that has earned its spot as a backpacker favorite. There's a small pool in the main courtyard with private rooms and dormitories surrounding it over three floors. On the top floor is an excellent bar that, thanks to its daily drink specials, gets jammed with backpackers and locals alike. On match days, it's soccer enthusiasts who cram the bar. In addition to on-site parties, the hostel organizes a wide array of outdoor adventures to the Sierra Nevada and rents out paddleboards for days at the beach.

Drop Bear Hostel (Cra. 21 No. 20-36, tel. 5/435-8034, www.dropbearhostel.com, COP$18,000 hammock, COP$25,000 dorm, COP$65,000 d) is a funky newcomer to the Santa Marta hostel scene. It's in a huge house that was built by a drug trafficker in the 1980s. Each night the Australian and New Zealander owners give tours of the house, including secret tunnels and nooks where money was stashed away. The bar is aptly named the Cartel Bar. Rooms are massive, and perhaps the nicest feature at Drop Bear is the big pool, which is the main gathering area at this sociable place.

COP$70,000-200,000

The Hotel del Parque (Cl. 19 No. 4-45, tel. 5/420-7508, COP$90,000 d) on the pleasant pedestrian Calle 19 is a gem of a find. Supremely low-key, this hotel has got just a handful of air-conditioned rooms, is very well maintained, and, best of all, it's fairly priced. There's complimentary coffee, but no free breakfast; however, there are many options within walking distance nearby.

Over COP$200,000

A Spanish couple has developed a small empire of boutique lodging and dining options in old Santa Marta. La Casa del Farol (Cl. 18 No. 3-115, tel. 5/423-1572, www.lacasadelfarol.com, COP$317,000 d) was their first, and one of the first boutique hotels in the city. It's in an 18th-century house and has six rooms that are named for different cities of the world. From the tiny wading pool on the rooftop you get a nice view of the city.

La Casa del Agua (Cl. 18 No. 4-09, tel. 5/423-1572, www.lacasadelagua.com.co, COP$225,000 d) is across the street from La Casa del Farol. It has four rooms of varying sizes and styles. Try for one with a balcony. The small pool downstairs is a welcome sight after a day out and about in the heat.

For some boutique pampering, try the 10-room Casa de Isabella (Callejón del Río, Cra. 2 No. 19-20, tel. 5/431-2082, cell tel. 301/466-5656, www.casaisabella.com, COP$250,000 d). It's a tastefully revamped republican-era house with nods to both colonial and republican styles, and it surrounds a tamarind tree that's over 200 years old. The suites on top have fantastic private terraces and hot tubs.

If you're more interested in a beach holiday, consider the beachfront Tamacá Beach Resort Hotel (Cra. 2 No. 11A-98, tel. 5/422-7015, www.tamaca.com.co, COP$315,000 d) in Rodadero. It has 81 rooms with all the usual amenities and a fantastic pool area that overlooks the water. The hotel has two towers, with the beachside tower preferred by most.

FOOD

Foodies from Europe and North America have converged on Santa Marta, making their dreams of opening up a restaurant become reality. And Samarians and travelers alike thank them.

There ought to be more restaurants like **(** Marisol (Cl. 19 No. 3-56, tel. 5/420-6511, www.marisolsantamarta.com, 8am-11pm daily, COP$18,000), an unpretentious spot that serves up healthy meals that are not too expensive, as well as deliciously fresh juices. It's run by a man from Cali who ran a successful restaurant in Berlin for many years. The location on the pedestrian Calle 19 is particularly peaceful, and you can grab a seat outside at night if you want. Sandwiches, pastas, and salads appear on the lunch and dinner menus. You can also grab a late breakfast here and chat with the servers if they're not busy.

For pizza the Sicilian way, look no further than La Pizzeria Italia Gourmet (Cra. 3A No. 16-24, tel. 5/422-7329, 5pm-11pm Mon.-Sat., COP$30,000) on the cute pedestrian alley, the Callejón del Correo. It's next door to the excellent Donde L'Italiano (Cra. 3A No. 16-26, cell tel. 316/429-1131, 5pm-11pm Mon.-Sat., COP$30,000) a cheerful restaurant where even the wallflower *pasta arrabiata* tastes exquisite. Go for a table in the courtyard in back.

An American-run place that delivers quality meals and drinks that will remind you of home is El Frescanjero (Cra. 7A No. 19-63, tel. 5/422-0379, 11am-2:30pm and 5:30pm-10:30pm Tues.-Sat., COP$20,000). They've got the most eclectic menu on the coast with Japanese chicken with ginger, vegetarian tacos, po'boys, and a platter of German sausage that automatically comes with a beer. And oh, the cocktail specials!

A locally run spot for a non-fussy, home-cooked meal is Mandragora (Cl. 20 No. 6-54, tel. 5/421-9392, cell tel. 301/400-3442, 11:30am-3pm Mon.-Sat., COP$12,000). Each day there is a set menu with fresh fish or typical Colombian dishes, such as *bandeja paisa* (dish of beans, various meats, yuca, and potatoes) on the menu.

For North Americans who've been on the road for a while, it's a treat to stumble upon **(** Agave Azul (Cl. 14 No. 3-58, tel. 5/431-6121, noon-10pm Tues.-Fri., 5pm-11pm Sat., COP$25,000). It's a Tex-Mex place, complete with margaritas, burritos, and nachos, in a space awash in warm colors. It's run by the same two American brothers who have **(** Ouzo (Cra. 3 No. 19-29, tel. 5/423-0658, 6pm-11pm Mon.-Sat., COP$25,000). Specializing in Mediterranean fare, Ouzo has brought some class to the park. Sizzling seafood or pasta accompanied by a glass of white wine will work out just fine for you. You can dine alfresco by candlelight if you wish, although you may be bothered by street vendors or beggars. It's not uncommon for visitors to hit both of these excellent restaurants in the same day.

The fab Restaurante Panamerican (Cl. 18 No. 1C-10, tel. 5/421-2901, noon-3pm and 6pm-10pm Mon.-Sat., noon-4pm Sun., COP$25,000) hasn't changed in decades—and why should it? While its heyday is long past, the Panamerican has an enormous menu specializing in steaks and seafood, but you can also just order a martini and enjoy the retro-chic atmosphere.

The way Samarios talk, it would seem that ❿ Donde Chucho (Cl. 6 at Cra. 3, tel. 5/422-1752, 11:30am-10:30pm daily, COP$25,000) is the only restaurant in Santa Marta and that it has been serving its mixed seafood platters since Bolívar was in town. It's in fast-moving Rodadero, and the open-air place is filled with photos of Chucho, the owner and chef, posing with Colombian beauty queens, sports stars, and the odd politician. It's hard to believe that Chucho began this seafood empire (he owns four restaurants now) with a humble wooden ceviche stand in Rodadero in the 1990s.

The terrace of Pepe Mar (Cra. 1 No. 6-05, Rodadero, tel. 5/422-2503, noon-10pm Tues.-Thurs. and Sun., until midnight Fri.-Sat., COP$26,000) is the best place for people-watching in all of Rodadero. Try the fried red snapper with coconut rice and, of course, a *patacón* (fried plantain) or two.

INFORMATION AND SERVICES

In addition to a stand at the airport, there is a PIT (Punto de Información Turística, Cra. 1 No. 10A-12, tel. 5/438-2587, 9am-noon and 2pm-6pm Mon.-Fri., 9am-1pm Sat.) tourist information booth along the waterfront.

Lavandería Paraíso (Cl. 22 No. 2A-46, tel. 5/431-2466, cell tel. 315/681-1651, 9am-6pm Mon.-Fri., 9am-1pm Sat.) will wash your clothes and have them ready for you to pick up by the next day. With

a little charm, you might be able to persuade them to have your things ready before 5pm the same day.

GETTING THERE AND AROUND

Santa Marta is easily accessed by air and by land from all major cities in Colombia.

The Aeropuerto Internacional Simón Bolívar (tel. 5/422-4604 or 5/422-4490) is 16 kilometers (10 miles) west of the *centro histórico*. Domestic carriers Avianca (www.avianca.com), LAN Colombia (www.lan.com), Viva Colombia (www.vivacolombia.com.co), and Easy Fly (www.easyfly.com.co) connect Santa Marta with the major cities of Colombia. Copa has nonstop flights to its hub in Panama City, Panama.

There is hourly bus service to Cartagena, Barranquilla, and Riohacha. Many buses to nearby coastal destinations leave from the market area in the *centro histórico*. Long-haul buses for destinations such as Bogotá, Medellín, and Bucaramanga depart from the Terminal de Transportes (Cl. 41 No. 31-17, tel. 5/430-2040) outside of town.

Taxis to Taganga cost around COP$8,000, and *colectivo* buses are around COP$1,200. These can be found on the waterfront near the Parque Bolívar, along Carrera 5, or at the market at Carrera 11 and Calle 11.

The best way to get around the *centro histórico* is on foot.

TAGANGA

This popular beachside community is only about a 20-minute ride through the desert to the northeast from Santa Marta and is actually considered part of the city. In the 1970s, this sleepy fishing village was discovered by hippie-types looking for an escape from urban life, and Taganga evolved into a mecca for backpackers. On any given Saturday along the bayside promenade, you'll brush shoulders with a truly mixed lot of humanity: Colombian families, diving fanatics, traveling musicians, and general sunseekers of all ages and nationalities. It's as close as Colombia gets to Venice Beach.

CARTAGENA

Recreation
DIVING AND SNORKELING

The warm waters (24-28°C/75-82°F) off of Taganga provide some good diving and snorkeling opportunities. Diving excursions take you into the waters off of the Parque Nacional Natural Tayrona to the northeast, the Isla Morro off the coast of Santa Marta, or to a shipwreck near the beaches of Rodadero. The best months for diving here are between July and September.

Run by a Paisa couple, Tayrona Dive Center (Cra. 1C No. 18A-22, tel. 5/421-5349, cell tel. 318/305-9589, www.tayronadivecenter.com, 8am-noon and 2pm-6pm daily) is a very organized agency that offers PADI certification courses (COP$650,000) over a period of three days with six dives each day, a one-day mini-course (COP$160,000), and diving excursions for those with experience. They also have a hotel (Cra. 1C No. 18A-22, tel. 5/421-5349, cell tel. 318/305-9589, www.tayronadivecenter.com, COP$40,000 pp) with eight rooms, five with views of the water.

Rooms have a safe deposit box and big refrigerators. The hotel is exclusively for divers during high season.

Oceano Scuba (Cra. 2 No. 17-46, tel. 5/421-9004, cell tel. 316/534-1834, www.oceanoscuba.com.co, 8am-noon and 2pm-6pm daily) offers the whole array of diving activities, from one-day dives for certified divers (COP$110,000) to a one-day beginner's course (COP$180,000) to an Open Water PADI certification course (COP$600,000) that lasts three days. Night dives (COP$80,000), during which you might come across eels hunting the waters, and snorkeling (COP$50,000) are also on offer.

BIKING AND TREKKING

Biking and hiking trips are the specialty of Elemento Outdoor Adventure (Cl. 18 No. 3-31, tel. 5/421-0870, cell tel. 310/605-0929, www.elementooutdoor.com, 8am-noon and 2pm-6pm Mon.-Fri., 9am-4pm Sat.-Sun.). Elemento offers a range of mountain bike adventures, including a

The fishing village of Taganga has become a backpacker mecca.

© ANDREW DIER

CARTAGENA

one-day downhill trip from Los Pinos to Minca (COP$140,000) with swimming hole stops along the way. There are also multi-day adventures in the area. For less adrenaline-pumping days, Elemento also offers visits to eco-farms, nature reserves, and indigenous communities.

BEACHES

There is a popular beach in front of the La Ballena Azul hotel, but the best beaches are a quick boat ride away. Beaches along the coast from Taganga to the Parque Nacional Natural Tayrona can be visited by boat. It costs about COP$40,000 round-trip to go to Tayrona from Taganga, but you can negotiate that price, especially if you are in a group. Although all visitors to the park are supposed to pay an entrance fee (and it is steep for non-Colombians), some boat captains will take you to beaches where no park employees will charge you for park entrance, which park officials rightly do not condone. During the windy months of December-February, boat transportation can be rough and dangerous.

Playa Grande is probably the best beach to visit, and it is one of the closest to Taganga. It costs COP$10,000 round-trip to get there by boat. To arrange for boat transportation to any of these beaches, just head to the beach in front of the promenade or at the La Ballena Azul. There are always boaters hanging about waiting for customers.

Accommodations

Owned by Olga from Bogotá, Hostal Pelikan (Cra. 2 No. 17-04, tel. 5/421-9057, cell tel. 316/756-1312, www.hostalpelikan.com, COP$25,000 dorm, COP$65,000 d) is a decent place to stay, with a nice terrace area for your morning coffee. Breakfast (with fruit!) is an additional fee.

The wooden cabins at La Casa del Profe (Cl. 21 No. 5A-36, cell tel. 311/882-8912, COP$50,000 pp) dot a mountain's edge and offer great views of the bay. There are eight rooms here, and guests may use the kitchen. It's about a 15-minute hike to the action in Taganga.

La Ballena Azul (Cra. 1 at Cl. 18, tel. 5/421-9009, www.hotelballenaazul.com, COP$173,000 d) is a Taganga classic, started by a Frenchwoman years ago. It's still in the family, and they still serve crêpes in their restaurant. Ballena Azul is on the beach, with the best location in town—in the center of activity.

Probably the most luxurious option in Taganga is the Hotel Bahía Taganga (Cl. 4 No. 1B-35, tel. 5/421-0653, cell tel. 310/216-9120, www.hotelbahiataganga.com, COP$235,000 d). It's on the eastern side of the bay. Head to the pool in the late afternoon and watch the sun slip behind the mountains.

Food

On the outdoor terrace of Bitacora (Cra. 1 No. 17-13, tel. 5/421-9482, 9am-11:30pm, COP$18,000) diners get front seat views to the boardwalk. Bitacora specializes in fresh, Taganga seafood, but there are also many vegetarian options as well as pastas. If you want to cool off with a coconut lemonade, this is the spot.

Babaganoush Restaurante y Bar (Cra. 1C No. 18-22, 3rd floor above Taganga Dive Center, cell tel. 318/868-1476, 1pm-11:30pm Wed.-Mon., COP$20,000) is an excellent Dutch-run restaurant and bar with amazing views. It's a true crowd pleaser with a diverse menu of falafels, seafood, steak, and even a shout-out to Southeast Asia. But surprisingly, you won't find any babaganoush! Go in the evening for the atmosphere, drinks, and sunsets. The daily happy hour is hard to pass up.

Getting There and Around

Taganga is easily reached from Santa Marta and from points east, such as the Parque Nacional Natural Tayrona and Palomino. Minibuses and buses ply that route daily. Minibuses from the *centro histórico* of Santa Marta depart from the market area on Carrera 5 and also from Carrera 1 near the Parque Simón Bolívar. The trip costs about COP$1,500. Taxis from Santa Marta cost around COP$12,000, more from the bus terminal or airport. Once in Taganga you can walk everywhere you need to go.

◖ MINCA

If you've had your fill of beaches or the seductive Caribbean cities, maybe it's time for an altitude adjustment. Artists, nature lovers, coffee farmers, and transplanted urbanites in the village of Minca (pop. 500) look down upon their neighbors in nearby Santa Marta—literally. At elevation of 660 meters, midway up the Sierra, you get a bird's-eye view of Santa Marta, just 45 minutes away. You also get a great bird's-eye view of birds, especially higher up at the edge of the Parque Nacional Sierra Nevada de Santa Marta. The blissful routine of mountain hikes, dips in invigorating swimming holes, and sunset ogling may make you want to linger here.

Recreation
HIKING

Minca is a paradise for those with a pair of hiking boots and a backpack slung over their shoulder. Hostels and hotels can point you in the right direction to several gentle hikes along tranquil mountain roads and paths to swimming holes of either

© ANDREW DIER

Peaceful and cool Minca is a nice break from the beach.

freezing cold or wonderfully refreshing pure water, depending on the thickness of your skin. Three popular walks with swimming holes are within easy walking distance from Minca: Balneario Las Piedras (45 mins.), Pozo Azul (1 hr.), and the Cascadas Marinka (1 hr.).

For a challenge, try the three-hour hike (one way) to the Los Pinos hostel at an elevation of 1,600 meters (5,250 feet). From there, or nearby, you can often get a fanastic glimpse of the snowcovered Pico Cristóbal Colón and Pico Bolívar, the highest mountain peaks in the country.

The Sierra Nevada de Santa Marta is a renowned coffee-growing region. The Finca La Victoria (no phone, 9am-4pm daily, COP$5,000) is a family-run coffee farm that you can visit for a small fee. It is between Pozo Azul and Los Pinos, about a one-hour walk from town.

In and around Minca there are no safety issues, and you can set off and up the mountain on your own without a guide.

BIRD-WATCHING

High into the Sierra Nevada, at an elevation of around 2,400 meters (7,875 feet), the Reserva El Dorado (www.proaves.org) is one of the finest bird-watching reserves in the country. For reservations (COP$569,000 3 nights all incl.), contact EcoTurs in Bogotá (Cra. 20 No. 36-61, tel. 1/287-6592, info@ecoturs.org) or Aviatur (tel. 1/587-5181, www.aviaturecoturismo.com) in Bogotá. The accommodations are excellent, with 10 spacious rooms, great food, and, crucially, hot showers. The area is home to 19 endemic species, including the Santa Marta antpitta, Santa Marta parakeet, Santa Marta bush tyrant, blossom crown, and screech owls. Anybody can stay at El Dorado, even the non-birding crowd.

Acccommodations
UNDER COP$70,000

◖ Oscar's Hostal Finca La Fortuna (400 m from town entrance near casino area, cell tel. 313/534-4500, http://hotelfincalafortuna.blogspot.com, COP$20,000 hammock, dorm COP$25,000,

COP$40,000 d) consists of simple and naturally luxurious cabins for a small capacity of guests dramatically set on a bluff with extraordinary views of Santa Marta and the surrounding countryside. Oscar's is completely off-grid, with solar panels providing electricity and rainwater collection and a well for all water use. Much of the land that you see from here (some 70 acres that is now a sea of trees) is owned by a man named Oscar, who is on a mission to undo some of the damage humans have done to the mountains of the Sierra Nevada through cattle ranching. The sunsets here, particularly from mid-June until mid-December, are "living art," as Oscar puts it. One- to two-day mule tours in the Sierra Nevada, with Oscar, can be arranged for COP$90,000 per day, per person. Reasonably priced breakfasts include homemade granola (COP$4,000), and other meals can be arranged as well.

Rancho de la Luna (300 m from town entrance near casino area, tel. 5/422-3160, cell tel. 317/249-7127, www.ranchodelalunaenminca.com, COP$70,000), in the countryside outside of Minca near Oscar's Hostal, is a guesthouse with two lodges with basic but very comfortable facilities (and great views of Santa Marta). But the real selling point is their wellness program: healthy food, massages, and yoga classes. These have additional costs, although there are packages that include yoga, a massage, meals, and two nights' accommodations for COP$200,000 pp.

El Mirador Hotel (200 m from town entrance, cell tel. 311/671-3456 or 318/368-1611, www.miradorminca.wordpress.com, COP$25,000 dorm, COP$45,000 d) is an enchanting hostel with a great view, warm hosts, and delicious meals. The hostel has three rooms, two private rooms and a dorm room with three beds. It's set in a lush garden, and the lovely dining area is open air. The restaurant is open to the public nightly and meals cost around COP$20,000.

Many travelers head up the mountain to spend some time at sociable Hostal Los Pinos (near Campano, cell tel. 313/587-7677 or 321/898-0641, lospinoshostal@yahoo.com, COP$20,000 dorm, COP$60,000 d). Hostal Los Pinos is on a mountain ridge (1,400 meters/4,600 feet) where the views are unbelievable. When it's clear, you can glimpse the snowcapped mountains of the Sierra Nevada. This is a fun spot, with lots of hanging around. There are some nice walks you can take from here, as well as high-adrenaline downhill bike rides, and hikes to waterfalls hidden in the mountains. And occasional paintball duels on-site.

COP$70,000-200,000

Operated by ProAves, the Hotel Minca (near town entrance, tel. 5/421-9958, cell tel. 317/437-3078, www.hotelminca.com, COP$135,000 d), once a convent, is one of the first hotels in Minca. There are 13 spacious rooms in this old-fashioned building with broad verandas with hammocks. There's a nature path on the grounds, and numerous hummingbird feeders along the open-air dining area ensure that you'll have a breakfast-time show.

Hostal Casa Loma (50 m uphill from the church, cell tel. 313/808-6134 or 321/224-6632, www.casalomaminca.com, COP$20,000 dorm, COP$80,000 d) is on a hilltop with a truly amazing vantage point over Santa Marta. It's a friendly place, where delicious food (often vegetarian) is served, and you mix and mingle with other travelers. Cabins farther on the hillside are quieter than the rooms near the main social area. Camping (COP$15,000) is also available. To get to Hostal Casa Loma, you must climb up a winding path just behind the town church. Casa Loma offers yoga classes (COP$20,000) on their forest terrace, massages (COP$55,000), and shows two films a week in their outdoor forest cinema.

Hostal Palo Alto (near Reserva El Dorado, cell tel. 300/642-1741 or 312/677-1403, www.tangaratours.co, tangaratours@gmail.com, COP$80,000 pp) is a mountain paradise, up high at an elevation of 1,700 meters, where you don't have to be a bird enthusiast to enjoy the crisp mountain air and natural beauty of the sierra—but if you are, this a great place to be. It's near the El Dorado bird-watching reserve. Accommodations here are basic, but comfortable.

Food

There are a handful of good eateries in Minca, mostly catering to international travelers. Hotels and hostels are always a reliable and reasonably priced option for guests and non-guests alike. They are open every day with lunch hours generally noon-3pm and dinner 6pm-10pm. Main dishes rarely cost more than COP$20,000. Standouts include Hostal Casa Loma (50 m above the church, cell tel. 313/808-6134 or 321/224-6632, www.casalomaminca.com), El Mirador Hotel (200 m from town entrance, cell tel. 311/671-3456 or 318/368-1611, www.miradorminca.wordpress.com), and Rancho de la Luna (300 m from town entrance near casino area, tel. 5/422-3160, cell tel. 317/249-7127, www.ranchodelalunaenminca.com).

Towards the church from the town entrance is Hola from La Sierra Café (town center, cell tel. 310/703-2870, holafromlasierracafe@gmail.com, 9am-9pm Wed.-Sun.). This friendly hippieish spot serves light and healthy meals, including breakfasts (pancakes!). They bake bread daily and also sell locally produced organic coffee and other products.

Bururake Fusion (town center, noon-3pm and 7pm-10pm Wed.-Sun., COP$18,000) has a daily menu and offers a little of everything: hamburgers, pastas, vegetarian dishes, and refreshing fruit juices. If you have the munchies after that morning hike, look for Empanadas Don Luis (no phone, 9am-7pm daily). They're the best.

Dining at El Mox Muica (300 m from town entrance, cell tel. 311/699-6718, 10am-9pm daily, COP$18,000) is like being invited to a friend's house. They only have two tables, candlelit at night, and these overlook a lush garden. The menu includes a variety of pastas, salads, crêpes, and wines. Andrea's specialty is cooking while Andrés is a woodcarver. With his father, accomplished painter and sculptor Manuel Bohorquez, he organizes woodcarving and ceramics workshops for visiting artists. Contact Andrés in advance for information at andresescultor@hotmail.com.

Information and Services

Bring plenty of cash with you to Minca: There are no ATMs here. There is a small tourist information stand (near police station, cell tel. 317/308-5270, 10am-6pm daily). It's run by the tour agency Jungle Joe's (www.junglejoeminca.com).

Getting There and Around

Minca is easily reached from Santa Marta. *Taxis colectivos* (shared taxis) depart on a regular basis from the market at Calle 11 and Carrera 12. These cost COP$7,000. Private taxis from the airport cost around COP$50,000 and taxis from the Centro cost COP$40,000.

◖ PARQUE NACIONAL NATURAL TAYRONA

Perhaps the best known national park in Colombia, the Parque Nacional Natural Tayrona (PNN Tayrona, 34 km northeast of Santa Marta on the Troncal del Caribe highway, tel. 5/421-1732, www.aviaturecoturismo.com or www.parquesnacionales.gov.co, 8am-5pm daily, COP$37,500 non-Colombian, COP$14,000 Colombian resident, COP$7,500 children, COP$7,500 students under age 25 with a valid ID) encompasses gorgeous beaches, tropical rainforests, and archaeological sites.

The park extends over 12,000 hectares (30,000 acres) of land from the edge of Taganga to the southwest to the Río Piedras on the east. The southern border of the park is the Troncal del Caribe highway and to the north is the Caribbean Sea. To the east and south of the PNN Tayrona is the PNN Sierra Nevada de Santa Marta, a much larger national park.

The frequently tempestuous waters of the PNN Tayrona provide dramatic scenery, with palms growing atop massive island boulders, waves crashing up against them. There are more than 30 golden sand beaches in the park that are set dramatically against a seemingly vertical wall of jungle. Although you can't see them from the park, the snow-covered peaks of the Sierra Nevada de

© ANDREW DIER

wild horses on the beach at the Parque Nacional Natural Tayrona

CARTAGENA

Santa Marta mountains are only 42 kilometers from the coast.

The park includes significant extensions of highly endangered dry tropical forests, mostly in the western section of the park. You will notice that these forests are much less dense than the humid tropical forests. At higher elevations you will see magnificent cloud forests. In addition to beaches, the coast includes marine estuaries and mangroves. The park includes streams with chilly waters that flow from high in the sierra: In the western part of the park, many of these run dry during the dry season, while in the eastern sector they have water year-round.

The forest in Parque Nacional Natural Tayrona is alive with plant and animal life. Over 1,300 plant, 396 bird, and 99 mammal species have been identified here. Four species of monkeys live in the park, and they can often be spotted. Five species of wild cats have been identified in the park. These are the margay, jaguar, ocelot, panther, and jaguarundi. Their numbers are few and these great cats are expert at hiding in the jungle: Don't count on stumbling across them during your visit! Other mammals include sloths, anteaters, armadillos, deer, and 40 types of bats. Birds include migratory and resident species, including the rare blue-billed curassow (locally called El Paujil), a threatened bird that lives in the cloud forest.

PLANNING YOUR TIME

There are two rainy seasons: April-June and September-November, with the latter more intense. During these times, trails can be extremely muddy. If at all possible, avoid visiting the PNN Tayrona during the high seasons mid-December through mid-January and Semana Santa, and to a lesser extent during the Colombian summer school holidays from mid-June until mid-July. During holidays the park is swarmed with visitors. Long holiday weekends (*puentes*) are also quite busy here, regular weekends less so, but during the week is by far the best. While many visit the park on daytrips from Santa Marta, spending one or two nights in the park is recommended, even though accommodations and food are expensive.

Recreation
BEACHES

The beaches in Parque Nacional Natural Tayrona are spectacular, but while the water may appear inviting, currents are deceivingly strong, and, despite the warnings posted on the beach, many people have drowned here. Of the park's 34 beaches, there are only 6 where you are allowed to swim. There are no lifeguards on duty in the park, and no specific hours for swimming. The best swimming beach is La Piscina, which is between the beaches of Arrecifes and Cabo San Juan (where you can also take a dip). To the west of Cabo San Juan is a clothing-optional beach. La Piscina is an inviting cove with crystal-clear waters. A natural rock barrier in the water keeps the waters always calm. It's a 20-minute walk west from Arrecifes.

Some of the other beaches open to swimming are in the less-visited western part of the park. Playa Neguanje is accessed by car or taxi (COP$15,000 from Santa Marta) through the Zalangana entrance (12 km northeast of Santa Marta). Playa del Muerto (Playa Cristal) is another recommended beach in the same area. It is over 20 kilometers from the entrance to the beach. You can visit some of the beaches on the western end of the park all the way to Cabo San Juan by boat from Taganga, but park staff prefer for visitors to enter the park by land. The waters can also be quite rough, especially between December and February.

HIKING

A highlight of any visit to the PNN Tayrona is the trek up to El Pueblito (also called Chairama, 3 km, 1.5 hrs. one way), which consists of ruins of what was an important Tayrona settlement. (Unless, that is, you have already visited the more impressive Ciudad Perdida site.) Here there are well-preserved remnants of terraces, and a small Kogi community still lives near the site. The somewhat challenging path through the tropical jungle is steep and the stone steps can be slippery, but it's well worth it. Hikers can go up to El Pueblito without a guide. El Pueblito is usually accessed from within Tayrona by walking west along the beach from the Arrecifes area. It can also be accessed from the main highway, the Troncal del Caribe.

At about 24 kilometers northeast of Santa Marta, ask to be let off at the Calabazo entrance to the park. It's about a 2.5-hour trek from there. It's not necessary, but if you'd like you can hire a guide to lead you to El Pueblito. Inquire about this when you check in.

Accommodations and Food

There are numerous lodging options in the PNN Tayrona for every budget, from the high-end Ecohabs to camping. The travel agency Aviatur (Bogotá office Av. 19 No. 4-62, tel. 1/587-5181 or 1/587-5182, www.aviaturecoturismo.com) manages most all lodging facilities in the park. Neither the Ecohabs nor the cabanas could be considered a bargain, but the Ecohabs, where you can awake to a beautiful view of the sea, are indeed special, and worth one or two nights. The cabanas are set back from the beach but are quite comfortable too.

The Ecohabs (COP$448,000 pp all meals incl.), in the Cañaveral sector, consist of 14 private *bohíos* (thatched-roof cabins) that, from a distance, look like giant nests amidst the trees. Really they are modeled after the thatched-roof houses of the Tayrona people. They sleep 2-4 persons. There are two floors to the Ecohabs. On the first floor is the bathroom and an open-air social area. On the second floor is the bedroom. A flashlight is necessary if you need to go to the bathroom in the middle of the night, as you have to go outside and downstairs. This is inconvenient for some.

In nearby Arrecifes, there are six two-story cabanas (12 rooms, COP$365,650 pp all meals incl.) with a capacity of four persons each. These are like jungle duplexes. The two units are divided by thin walls. There is also a hammock area (COP$23,000 pp) in Arrecifes with a capacity of 60 hammocks. For those choosing this option, there are lockers and you can lock things in the safety box at the lobby area.

There are campgrounds (COP$15,000 pp) in both Cañaveral and Arrecifes and also at Cabo San Juan, which is a 15-minute walk to the west from the beach at La Piscina. It tends to get very crowded, bordering on unpleasant, during long weekends and holidays.

Safety boxes are included in all rooms, and can be provided to campers as well. That said, some prefer to leave a bag or valuables at a trusted hotel in Santa Marta.

The park has two restaurants in Cañaveral, close to the Ecohabs, and in Arrecifes near the cabanas. They are open every day 7am-9pm, and the specialty here is fresh seafood. Expect to pay around COP$30,000 for a lunch or dinner entrée. There are some snack bars in the park as well.

Getting There and Around

From Santa Marta you can take any bus eastbound along the Troncal del Caribe to the main entrance (Zaino Gate). *Colectivo* buses can be caught at the intersection of Carrera 11 and Calle 11 (the market) in Santa Marta, and the trip takes about an hour and costs under COP$5,000. You can also take a cab for about COP$60,000.

There is usually an extremely thorough inspection of backpacks and bags upon entering the park. Visitors are not allowed to bring in plastic bags (to protect sea turtles) and no alcohol (although it is served at restaurants and snack bars in the park). Be sure to bring bug repellent, a flashlight, and good hiking boots.

At the administrative offices, visitors pay entrance fees. These fees are not included in the Aviatur package prices. Although technically park visitors are supposed to carry proof of a yellow fever vaccination, this is rarely, if ever, checked.

It's about four kilometers from the offices to Cañaveral, and vans make this route on an ongoing basis (COP$2,000). From there it is a sweaty 45 more minutes on foot through the jungle to Arrecifes. Mules can be hired to carry your bags, or you can rent a horse for COP$20,000.

PNN TAYRONA TO PALOMINO

If you prefer less civilization and more tranquility, the coast between PNN Tayrona and Palomino has some interesting places to hang your *sombrero vueltiao* (Colombian hat) for a few days. Between these two very popular tourist destinations, there are beaches that are rather overlooked by the masses. Day trips to PNN Tayrona can be easily coordinated from this area.

Impossibly placed upon giant beach boulders, the guesthouse Finca Barlovento (Playa Los Naranjos to the east of PNN Tayrona, Bogotá tel. 1/325-6998, www.fincabarloventosantamarta.com, COP$400,000 d incl. 2 meals) is located between the sea and the Río Piedras. It's an amazing place to stay, and the food's good, too. There are just three rooms and one more luxurious cabin here. Jungle excursions can be arranged by the hotel, but you'll want to enjoy some beachside afternoons. You'll have the beach to yourself.

Self-described as "chilled out," Costeño Beach Surf Camp and Ecolodge (Playa Los Naranjos, cell tel. 310/368-1191, www.costenosurf.com, COP$30,000 dorm, COP$80,000 d) gets exceptionally high marks from its guests for its laid-backness. And while you don't have to be a surfer or skater to fit in here, it doesn't hurt either. Boards are rented for COP$30,000 per day, and classes cost COP$25,000. Costeño Beach has both dorm and private accommodations on this former coconut farm. It's also solar powered.

Playa Koralia (48 km east of Santa Marta, cell tel. 310/642-2574 or cell tel. 317/510-2289, www.koralia.com, COP$209,000 d) is a beach-chic hotel on the beach just east of the Parque Nacional Natural Tayrona. It's rustic: There is no electricity. Candlelit meals (always vegetarian-friendly), star-gazing, an evening drink by the bonfire, and a little spa time are Playa Koralia's recipe for peace.

PALOMINO

Swaying coconut palms and uncrowded beaches: That's what the Caribbean is all about, isn't it? And at Palomino that's exactly what you get. This town on the Troncal del Caribe is just across the border in the La Guajira department. And it's become quite a popular destination, particularly with backpackers. Caribbean currents can be frustratingly strong here, but the cool waters of the nearby Río Palomino flowing down from the Sierra Nevada de Santa Marta are always refreshing and much more hospitable towards visitors. Palomino is a good stop to make between Santa Marta and desert adventures in the Alta Guajira.

Recreation

Recreational activities in and around Palomino include easy day trip walks to the Río Palomino, about an hour away, where there is also tubing. This river forms the eastern border of the town. Also in the area are the fantastic jungle waterfalls at Quebrada Valencia (between PNN Tayrona and Palomino). All hotels and hostels organize these easy excursions. Samarian families visit these swimming holes to cool off on the weekends.

Chajaka (office on the south side of the main coastal highway, cell tel. 313/583-3288) offers interesting day trips or multi-day hiking trips (COP$120,000) into the Sierra Nevada to visit Kogui communities and experience the jungle.

Shivalila Yoga (La Sirena hostel, cell tel. 321/450-7359, yogashivalila@gmail.com, COP$15,000 class) offers yoga classes at the crunchy La Sirena hostel on the beach. Inquire at the hostel for the weekly schedule.

Accommodations and Food

Palomino is well on its way to dethroning Taganga as the deluxe backpacker resort. That's thanks largely to one famous hostel: The Dreamer (Palomino, cell tel. 300/609-7229, www.thedreamerhostel.com, COP$29,000 dorm, COP$110,000 d). This is by far the most social option this side of Santa Marta. Dorm and private accommodations are in *malokas* (cabins) surrounding an always-happening pool area and outdoor snack bar.

Next door to The Dreamer is Cabañas San Sebastián (Palomino, cell tel. 300/432-7170 or cell tell. 310/775-4630, www.sansebastianpalomino.com.co, COP$30,000 pp). It consists of two cabins and three rooms for rent, just a few meters from the beach.

Don't miss the excellent juice stand at the beach in front of The Dreamer, where friendly Alejandro even has his own organic chocolate for sale.

At the Hotel Hukumeizi (Palomino, cell tel. 315/354-7871 or 317/566-7922, www.turismoguajira.com, info@hukumeizi.com, COP$250,000 pp all meals) there are 16 cute, round *bohíos* (bungalows) with a restaurant in the center. If you go during the week, you'll probably have the place to yourselves, but service may be less attentive. From here it's about a 15-minute walk along the beach to the Río San Salvador and about an hour from the Río Palomino.

El Matuy (Donde Tuchi) (Palomino, cell tel. 315/751-8456, www.elmatuy.com, COP$180,000 pp including meals) is a privately owned nature reserve with 10 cabins amid the palms and no electricity (this means candlelight evenings and no credit card machine). Hotel staff can help organize horseback riding or other activities. Food is varied, yet portions are not extremely generous.

On the Troncal del Caribe, the Hostal Mochileros Culturart (Cl. 1B No. 4-25, cell tel. 312/626-6934) is a cultural center for Palomino, where there are often musical performances and other events in the evenings. There is a restaurant here with fine veggie burgers and refreshing juices, and, as the name suggests, there are rooms available at this hostel.

Getting There and Around

There is regular bus transportation along the Troncal del Caribe between Santa Marta and Riohacha. Take a bus bound for Palomino from Santa Marta at the market on Carrera 11 and Calle 11. It's about a two-hour trip. It costs COP$10,000. On the highway where the bus drops you off, there are young men on motorbikes who will take you to your hotel (COP$3,000) on the beach.

PARQUE NACIONAL NATURAL SIERRA NEVADA DE SANTA MARTA

Encompassing almost the entire Sierra Nevada mountain range is the Parque Nacional Natural Sierra Nevada de Santa Marta (www.parquesnacionales.gov.co). This park has a total area of 383,000 hectares (945,000 acres), making it one of the larger parks in Colombia.

The main attraction is the Ciudad Perdida (Lost City), the most important archaeological site of the Tayrona, the pre-Columbian civilization that inhabited the Sierra Nevada. The Tayrona had a highly urbanized society, with towns that included temples and ceremonial plazas built on stone terraces. There are an estimated 200 Tayrona sites, but Ciudad Perdida is the largest and best known. Many of these towns, including Pueblito (in the Parque Nacional Natural Tayrona), were occupied at the time of the Spanish conquest. Today, an estimated 30,000 indigenous people who are descendants of the Tayronas, including the Kogis, Arhuacos, Kankuamos, and Wiwas, live on the slopes and valleys of the Sierra Nevada de Santa Marta. These people believe that the Sierra Nevada is the center of the universe and that the mountain's health controls the entire Earth's well-being. Many areas of the sierra are sacred sites to these people and are barred to outsiders.

The Sierra Nevada de Santa Marta mountain range is best described as a giant pyramid, which is bordered on the north by the Caribbean and on the southeast and southwest by the plains of northern Colombia. Although some believe that the range is a distant extension of the Cordillera Oriental (Eastern Mountain Range) of the Andes, most geologists believe it is a completely independent mountain system.

It is the world's highest coastal mountain range, with the twin peaks of Pico Cristóbal Colón and Pico Bolívar (the two are called Chinundúa by indigenous groups in the area) reaching 5,776 meters (18,950 feet; Colón is said to be slightly higher than Bolívar) but located only 42 kilometers from the sea. Pico Cristóbal Colón is the world's fifth most prominent mountain after Mount Everest (Nepal/Tibet, China), Mount Aconcagua (Argentina), Mount McKinley (U.S.), and Mount Kilimanjaro (Tanzania). In addition, there are seven other snow-covered peaks that surpass 5,000 meters: Simonds, La Reina, Ojeda, Los Nevaditos, El Guardián, Tulio Ospina, and Codazzi. Treks to these peaks used to be possible from the northern side of the mountains, starting at the Arhuaco indigenous village of Nabusimake (Cesar), but are no longer permitted by the indigenous communities.

The PNN Sierra Nevada de Santa Marta encompasses the entire mountain range above 600 meters (16,400 feet). In addition, a small segment of the park east of the PNN Tayrona, from the Río Don Diego to the Río Palomino, extends to sea level. This means that the park encompasses the entire range of tropical ecosystems in Colombia, from low-lying tropical forests (sea level to 1,000 meters), cloud forests (1,000-2,300 meters), high mountain Andean forest (2,300-3,500 meters), *páramo* (highland moor, 3,500-4,500 meters), super *páramo* (4,500-5,000 meters), and glaciers (above 5,000 meters). However, because access to the upper reaches of the park is limited, what visitors will most be able to appreciate is low-lying tropical and cloud forest.

The isolation of the range has made it an island of biodiversity, with many plant and animal species found nowhere else. The Sierra Nevada de Santa Marta is home to 187 mammal species, including giant anteaters, spider monkeys, peccaries, tree rats, jaguars, and pumas. There are 46 species of amphibians and reptiles, including several that live above 3,000 meters that are found nowhere else on the planet. There are an astonishing 628 bird species, including the Andean condor, blue-knobbed curassow, sapphire-bellied hummingbird, and black-solitary eagle, as well as many endemic species. There are at least 71 species of migratory birds that travel between Colombia and North America.

CARTAGENA

COURTESY OF JAY SPELLER, CASA LOMA IN MINCA

the mystical Ciudad Perdida

🄲 Ciudad Perdida Trek

A highlight for many visitors to Colombia is the four- to six-day, 52-kilometer (32-mile) round-trip trek to the Ciudad Perdida (Lost City) in the Sierra Nevada mountains of the Caribbean coast. The Ciudad Perdida is within the confines of the Parque Nacional Natural Sierra Nevada de Santa Marta.

The Ciudad Perdida, called Teyuna by local indigenous tribes and Buritaca 200 by archaeologists, was a settlement of the Tayrona, forebears of the people who inhabit the Sierra Nevada today. It was probably built starting around AD 700, at least 600 years before Machu Picchu. There is some disagreement as to when it was abandoned: There is evidence of human settlement until the 16th century. The site was visited in the early 1970s by *guaqueros* (treasure hunters) who pillaged the site. News of its discovery in 1976 marked one of the most important archaeological events of recent years. From 1976 to 1982, archaeologists from the Colombian National Institute of History and Anthropology painstakingly restored the site.

Spread over some 35 hectares (86 acres), the settlement consists of 169 circular terraces atop a mountain in the middle of dense cloud forest. Archaeologists believe that this sophisticated terrace system was created in part to control the flow of water in this area known for torrential rainfall for much of the year.

Plazas, temples, and dwellings for tribal leaders were built on the terraces in addition to an estimated 1,000 *bohíos* (traditional thatched roof huts), which housed between 1,400 and 3,000 people. A fire was always at the center of the *bohío*, and there was a domestic area where food and water were stored and cooking took place, as well as an artisan area for goldsmithing.

Surrounding the Ciudad Perdida were farms of coca, tobacco, pumpkin, and fruit trees. The city was connected to other settlements via an intricate system of mostly stone paths.

The hike is, by and large, uphill, as you reach an elevation of 1,100 meters (3,600 feet). There are nearly 20 river crossings to be made. Towards the end of the third day, you will climb about 1,200 often treacherously slippery stone steps until you reach the spectacular terraces of Ciudad Perdida. For many this sight makes all the sweat, fatigue, and mosquito bites worthwhile.

There is one set fee (COP$600,000) for the trek. This does not change, no matter if you're making the trek in three, four, or five days. If you are in very good shape and prefer taking the Ciudad Perdida express route, the trek can be done in three nights and four days. This requires six hours hiking per day and rising early. For some, the long nights of card playing at campsites can get old quick; others enjoy the camaraderie with hikers from all over the world. In case of an emergency on the mountain, a burro or helicopter will be sent to retrieve the hiker, for a fee.

It's important to only go with a reputable tour company, such as Magic Tour (Cl. 16 No. 4-41, Santa Marta, tel. 5/421-5820; Cl. 14 No. 1B-50, Taganga, tel. 5/421-9429; www.magictourcolombia. com) or TurCol (Cl. 13 No. 3-13, Centro Comercial San Francisco Plaza, Local 115, Santa Marta; Cl. 19 No. 5-40, Taganga, tel. 5/421-2556; www.turcol. com or www.buritaca200.com). A third option is Baquianos Tour (Cl. 10C No. 1C-59, Santa Marta, tel. 5/431-9667, www.lostcitybaquianos.com). Your tour company will provide food (advise in advance if you have special dietary needs or wants), hammocks or cots with mosquito netting, and mules to carry up supplies.

You'll need to bring a small to medium-sized backpack, enough to carry a few days of clothes, good hiking boots with strong ankle support, sandals for stream crossings (keeping your boots dry), long pants, mosquito repellent, water purifying tablets, sunscreen, cash for refreshments to purchase along the way, a small towel, toilet paper, hand sanitizer, flashlight, sealable bags to keep things dry, light rain jacket, and a water container. If you have them, trekking poles may be a nice addition. Sleeping bags may provide more comfort at night but aren't necessary.

From mid-December through mid-January you'll have plenty of company along the way: It's high tourist season. Other high seasons are during Semana Santa and June-July. The wettest months tend to be April-May and September-November. Expect a daily downpour and doable, but sometimes rather treacherous, river crossings during those times of the year. When it's raining or has been raining, the trek is more challenging. On the plus side, there are usually fewer crowds on the mountain at that time.

Campsites along the way turn into backpacker villages during high seasons, but they never turn in to rowdy scenes by any means. Upon arrival the routine is fairly standard. You'll often be able to cool off in the pristine waters of nearby swimming holes, have dinner, and hit the hammocks. Sleeping in hammocks can be uncomfortable for those not used to them. Earplugs come in handy for light sleepers.

The trek begins at the settlement of Mamey on the Río Buritaca. Along the way you will no doubt come in contact with Kogi people who live in the Sierra Nevada, and will pass through the village of Mutanyi. These lands are theirs and visitors are encouraged to refrain from taking photographs of them without prior permission. One of the most popular tourist activities in Colombia, the trek is considered quite safe.

Estación San Lorenzo

Deeper and higher into the Sierra Nevada de Santa Marta from the town of Minca and set amid pristine cloud forest is the Estación San Lorenzo (Santa Marta parks office, Cl. 17 No. 4-06, tel. 5/423-0752 or 5/421-3805, sierranevada@parquesnacionales.gov.co, 8am-noon and 2pm-6pm Mon.-Fri.; Bogotá parks office, tel. 1/353-2400, www.parquesnacionales.gov.co), part of the Parque Nacional Natural Sierra Nevada de Santa Marta. At this spot at 2,200 meters (7,200 feet) in the Sierra Nevada, visitors can make guided walks through the cloud forest to see birds and enjoy views of the snow-covered peaks in the park. The two cabins (COP$25,000-35,000 pp) of San Lorenzo are wonderfully isolated amid the forest.

A stay here can be an inexpensive way to get to know the Sierra Nevada, but there are many hoops you must go through to arrange it. First you must contact the parks office, preferably in Santa Marta, to inquire about availability. Then you will be required to make a *consignación* (deposit) to their bank account to cover the cost of your stay. This involves filling out a deposit form and standing in line at their bank (Banco de Bogotá).

The easiest way to get to San Lorenzo is by *mototaxi* from Minca, and this can cost around COP$50,000. Alternatively, and if you are traveling in a small group, it may make sense to arrange transportation with an SUV, which can cost up to COP$250,000.

Accommodations are basic here, and there are just two cabins, each with three rooms holding six beds each, for a total capacity of 36. No meals are provided here, but there is a rustic kitchen facility with basic utensils and cooking implements. You will have to provide your own propane gas canister (readily available in Santa Marta) and all your food for cooking. The temperature drops significantly in the evening, thus it is important to bring warm clothes. There is a fireplace in both cabins.

La Guajira

The vast Guajira Peninsula has some of the most rugged, beautiful landscapes in Colombia. It is home to the Wayúu indigenous people, who have maintained their independent way of life through centuries. Though many Wayúu now live in cities and towns, their traditional *rancherías* (settlements) dot the desert. With the growth of tourism, many have set up lodging using traditional *ranchería* houses made out of *yotojoro,* the dried hearts of cactus plants.

The Colombian side of the peninsula (Venezuela shares the other part) can be divided into three sections. The Baja Guajira (Lower Guajira), near the Sierra Nevada de Santa Marta, is fertile agricultural and cattle-ranching land. The much more arid middle swath, with the departmental capital of Riohacha and the unlovely towns of Uribia and Maicao, is home to the majority of the population. The Alta Guajira (Upper Guajira), from Cabo de la Vela to Punta Gallinas, is sparsely populated and has some truly otherworldly landscapes. Focus your visit on this last part.

Lack of infrastructure, especially in the north, makes visiting the Guajira a challenge, so most people opt for organized tours. Though it is possible to get to Cabo de la Vela on public transportation, do not travel elsewhere in the Alta Guajira without a dependable local guide. The roads are

unmarked tracks in the sand, and getting lost is inevitable. More urgently, in this somewhat lawless place, where the Colombian government has limited authority, there are unscrupulous people ready to prey on unsuspecting visitors.

During the rainy months September to November, it can be difficult to travel through the desert, which can become muddy to the point of impassable.

History

Spanish navigator Juan de la Cosa, who was a member of Columbus's first three voyages, disembarked in Cabo de la Vela in 1499, making the Guajira Peninsula one of the first places visited by Europeans in South America. It was not until 1535 that explorer Fernando de Enciso founded a settlement near Cabo de la Vela, which became a center of pearl extraction. This early settlement was relocated to Riohacha, which was founded in 1544. The traditional Wayúu inhabitants of the peninsula put up strong resistance to Spanish advances. During the 19th and 20th centuries, the peninsula was used primarily as a smuggling route.

For better or for worse, the fortunes of the Guajira changed in 1975 when the Colombian government entered into an agreement with oil giant

Exxon to develop the Cerrejón open-pit coal mine 80 kilometers (50 miles) southeast of Riohacha. This project involved the construction of Puerto Bolívar, a coal port located in Bahía Portete, and of a railway to transport the coal. Production started in 1985. Coal has since become one of Colombia's main exports. The mine has generated more than US$2 billion in royalties for the Colombian government. Little of this wealth has trickled down to the people of La Guajira. It is the fourth poorest department in Colombia.

RIOHACHA

Called Süchiimma in the Wayúu language, meaning "city of the river," Riohacha (pop. 231,000) is La Guajira's slow-paced departmental capital. It is one of the oldest cities in Colombia. Not a tourist destination itself, Riohacha is an excellent base from which to launch tours of Alta Guajira.

Sights

Along Calle 1, also known as Avenida Marina, is the Paseo de la Playa boardwalk, where locals and tourists take their evening strolls and take in the sea air. Along the way are kiosks where vendors sell ceviches and Wayúu women set up their brightly colored *mochilas* (traditional woven handbags) on the sidewalk, nonchalantly waiting for customers. The kilometer-long pier known as the Muelle Turístico is another favorite place for a walk. There are no railings, so maybe those who have had a couple of drinks should sit this one out.

Parque Padilla (Cl. 2 and Cra. 7), Riohacha's shady main plaza, is named after favorite son Admiral José Prudencio Padilla, who was the most prominent Afro-Colombian commander in the revolutionary wars. To one side of the plaza is the only remnant of colonial Riohacha, the heavily reconstructed Catedral de Nuestra Señora

© ANDREW DIER

the endless deserts of La Guajira

de los Remedios (Cl. 2 No. 7-13, tel. 5/727-2442, masses 6:30am and 7pm Mon.-Sat., 7am, 11am, and 7pm Sun.), originally erected in the 16th century. The remains of Padilla repose there.

On the Riohacha-Maicao road just outside of town is the Sendero Eco-Cultural El Riíto (no phone, 7am-6pm daily), a pleasant nature walk where you can observe birds that was completed in 2013. This is a great place to stretch your legs before or after a long and bumpy ride through the desert.

Accommodations and Food

Riohacha isn't known for fantastic lodging or dining, but then again you will probably be spending limited time here.

The Hotel Castillo del Mar (Cra. 9A No. 15-352, tel. 5/727-5043, cell tel. 316/525-1295, hotel-castillodelmar@gmail.com, COP$25,000 dorm, COP$100,000 d) is about a 10-minute walk from the boardwalk in a quiet residential area. It's the choice of backpackers. There are 11 rooms, some with air conditioning, some without. It could be

more comfortable, but for the price it's a bargain.

Closer to downtown, the Hotel Arimaca (Cl. 1 Av. La Marina No. 8-75, tel. 5/727-3515, www.hotelarimaca.com, COP$130,000 d) will do for a night. It has 50 rooms and caters to the business crowd during the week. Oceano (Cra. 15 No. 9-21, tel. 5/728-1108, www.oceanohotel.co, COP$140,000 d) has 15 rooms and is a couple of blocks from the boardwalk.

Taroa Lifestyle Hotel (Cl. 1 No. 4-77, tel. 5/729-1122, www.taroahotel.com, COP$200,000) is the first so-called "Wayúu lifestyle hotel" in Colombia, and it opened in July 2013. It is only about half an hour to the northeast. It's on the beach and has 46 rooms.

There are several seafood restaurants along Avenida Marina. Try the Casa del Marisco (Cl. 1 4-43, tel. 5/728-3445, 10am-10pm daily, COP$25,000), a restaurant that serves an array of fresh seafood dishes and pastas.

For for a wider range of dishes, try Sazón Internacional (Cl. 1 No. 3-57, tel. 5/728-0415, noon-10pm Tues.-Sun.). For something quick go to the food court of the modern Centro Comercial Suchiimma (Cl. 15 No. 8-56, 10am-9pm daily). There are some vegetarian options available here, and at the Jumbo store, you can pick up all the provisions you need for a long ride through the desert.

Getting There and Around

Aeropuerto Almirante Padilla (Cl. 29B No. 15-217, tel. 5/727-3854) is five minutes north of town. There are only one or two flights per day from Bogotá to Riohacha on Avianca (ticket office Cl. 7 No. 7-04, tel. 5/727-3624, www.avianca.com, 8am-6pm Mon.-Fri., 9am-1pm Sat.). On Tuesdays and Saturdays, Tiara Air Aruba (Cl. 2 No. 6-64, Local 2, tel. 5/727-3737, www.tiara-air.com, 8am-noon and 2pm-6pm Mon.-Fri.) operates flights between Riohacha and Aruba, with connections to and from Fort Lauderdale.

The bus station (Av. El Progreso and Cl. 11) has frequent services to Maicao, Santa Marta, and Barranquilla. There are also services to Valledupar, Cartagena, and Bogotá. Shared taxis to Uribia, where you can pick up trucks to Cabo de la Vela, leave from Calle 15 and Carrera 1.

The center of town, along the boardwalk, is easily walkable.

BORDER CROSSING

For stays under 90 days, U.S., Canadian, and most European citizens do not require a visa to enter Venezuela. You may be required to show proof of a hotel reservation and proof of an air ticket departing from Venezuela, and your passport must not expire within six months of entry into Venezuela. There is a Venezuelan consulate in Riohacha for further queries: Consulado de Venezuela (Cra. 7 No. 3-08, Edificio El Ejecutivo, Piso 2, tel. 5/727-4076, 8am-noon and 2pm-5pm Mon.-Thurs., 8am-1pm Fri.). There is an entry point to Venezuela at the town of Maicao.

SANTUARIO DE FAUNA Y FLORA LOS FLAMENCOS

Any day you see a pink flamingo is a good day. That's enough of a reason to visit the Santuario de Fauna y Flora Los Flamencos (Camarones, cell tel. 301/675-3862 or 313/514-0366, ecoturismosantuario@gmail.com, www.parquesnacionales.gov.co, free). This park is 25 kilometers southwest of Riohacha and is home to thousands of *Phoenicopterus ruber ruber* or American flamingos. The 700-hectare sanctuary, which is part of the national park system, encompasses a magnificent coastal estuary where the flamingos fish for shrimp in the shallow waters.

To get there, you can take a bus from Riohacha going towards Camarones or points southwest. From Camarones take a *mototaxi* to the entrance of the park (COP$2,000). To see the flamingos up close, take a *chalupa* (wooden boat) onto the lagoon (COP$15,000 for two people). To avoid the glaring sun, visit the park early in the morning or late in the afternoon.

At the Centro de Visitantes Los Mangles (cell tel. 301/675-3862 or 313/514-0366, ecoturismosantuario@gmail.com, COP$100,000 meals and tours) there are five tiny yet spic and span cabins that can be rented, and there is an area for sleeping in *chinchoros* (large hammocks; COP$20,000). These are located between the bay and the sea. In addition to the flamingos, the beach at the park is quite nice and you can take an excursion through the mangroves. It's a charming place, and is a good option if you'd prefer not to stay in Riohacha.

◖ ALTA GUAJIRA

The Alta Guajira (Upper Guajira) comprises the entire peninsula east of Cabo de la Vela and Uribia. It is very sparsely populated: The three largest settlements, where most of the tourism infrastructure is located, are Cabo de la Vela, Punta Gallinas at the very northern tip, and Nazareth, in the northeast. The terrain has a striking ochre color, with rocky and sandy patches. The vegetation is mostly shrubs and cacti. The Caribbean coast here is broken by three large bays with stunning turquoise and aquamarine waters: Bahía Portete, Bahía Honda, and Bahía Hondita. The last of these is easily accessible to tourists in day trips from Punta Gallinas. There are a few low mountain ranges, including the Serranía de la Macuira (864 meters/2,835 feet), located in the extreme northeastern corner of the peninsula, but overall the terrain is low and slightly undulated.

The only destination in the Alta Guajira that is accessible by public transportation is Cabo de la Vela. Though it is possible to contract transportation by land or sea to Punta Gallinas, most visitors opt to visit the region in an easily organized tour.

The sands of Alta Guajira are a favorite location for raucous 4x4 races and competitions. A large annual event is the Rally Aventura Guajira (www. ruedalibrexcolombia.net), which takes place in August, when more than 200 vehicles trek across the desert from Riohacha to Cabo de la Vela. If this isn't your bag you may want to double-check your dates of travel to make sure they don't coincide with the event.

Tours

The standard Alta Guajira tour involves going to Cabo de la Vela on day one, with a stop at the now-abandoned salt mines of the Salinas de Manaure (not worth a visit), spending the night at Cabo de la Vela, continuing on the next day to Punta Gallinas, and returning to Riohacha on day three (COP$340,000-380,000 per person, including food and lodging). A longer tour involves two additional nights in Nazareth to visit the Parque Natural Nacional Macuira (COP$800,000-880,000 per person, including food and lodging).

Make sure to check how many people are in your SUV, as there have been reports of tour operators who cram seven people into a vehicle, making for an uncomfortable ride. Tour guides generally have a limited grasp of English.

The most comfortable option by far is to rent an SUV with a driver for your own party. This costs around COP$400,000 per day, not including food and lodging.

The desert countryside seems endless and is beautiful in its own desolate way. You'll be amazed at how these drivers know which way to go, as there are no road signs, only cacti and occasional goats. Every once in a while, you will have to pay "tolls" to

Wayúu children who have set up quasi road blocks. To gain their permission to cross, drivers hand over crackers, cookies, or candy.

TOUR COMPANIES

Tour companies offer package tours or private vehicles. A highly recommended tour company is Expedición Guajira (Cl. 2 No. 5-06, tel. 5/727-2336, cell tel. 311/439-4677 or 301/464-2758, franklin_penalver@yahoo.com), managed by Franklin Penalver. His guides, of Wayúu origin, know the area like the back of their hands.

Solera Travels (Cra. 9A No. 15-352, cell tel. 316/525-1295, gerenciacomercial@soleratravels. com) has an office at the Castillo de Mar hostel and sells all the regular tour packages. Kaishi (Plaza Principal, Uribia, cell tel. 311/429-6315, www.kai-shitravel.com) is another agency that has a good reputation.

CABO DE LA VELA

Cabo de la Vela (known as Jepira in the Wayúu language), 180 kilometers north of Riohacha, is a small Wayúu fishing village spread along the Caribbean Sea. It comes as a shock—a pleasant one—after several hours driving through the arid landscape to finally arrive at the waters of the Caribbean. Here the beaches are nice, the views otherworldly, and the atmosphere peaceful. The smooth waters and ample winds provide near perfect conditions for windsurfing and kite surfing, and Cabo de la Vela has become a destination for these sports.

There are several pleasant excursions near town, and if you take an organized package tour, all of these should be included in the price. One is to El Faro, a lighthouse on a high promontory with spectacular nearly 360-degree views of the surrounding ocean. Another is to the Ojo del Agua, a small but pleasant beach near a freshwater spring. Farther afield is the Pilón de Azúcar, a high hill that affords incredible views to the surrounding region. Nearby is the Playa de Pilón, a beautiful ochre-colored beach. To the west is the Jepirachi Wind Farm, the first of its kind of Colombia; the

© ANDREW DIER

Cabo de la Vela, La Guajira

turbines make for a somewhat surreal sight in the midst of this barren territory. Organized tours include stops at these spots. If you are on your own, hotels can organize these excursions for you. Trips to these sights in SUVs cost around COP$15,000 per person, round-trip, with a minimum of two persons.

Recreation

Cabo de la Vela is an excellent place to practice or learn how to kite or windsurf. Eoletto (Ranchería Utta, cell tel. 321/468-0105 or 314/851-6216, www.windsurfingcolombia.com) is a windsurfing and kitesurfing school run by Etto from Germany. An eight-hour windsurfing course costs COP$380,000; kitesurfing is COP$900,000. Rentals are available for COP$50,000 per hour.

Accommodations

Family-run guesthouses are plentiful in Cabo de la Vela, and are quite rudimentary. Freshwater is always scarce here in the desert, so long showers are not an option. Floors are usually sandy, and electricity is limited. The street in Cabo de la Vela along the sea is lined with about 15 guesthouses. There are a few lodgings outside of town towards El Faro, such as Rancheria Utta.

The Rancheria Utta (300 m northwest of town, Vía al Faro, cell tel. 312/687-8237 or 313/817-8076, www.rancheriautta.com, COP$15,000 hammock, COP$35,000 bed pp) is a nice place to stay. It is just far enough from the village of Cabo de la Vela that you can experience the magical ambience of being far away from civilization. Cabins are simple with walls made from the hearts of *yotojoro* (cacti). That is a traditional form of construction in the desert. There are 11 *cabañas* with a total of 35 beds and plenty of inviting *chinchorros* (hammocks) for lazing about. Being on the beach at night, looking up at the stars and listening to the sound of gentle waves breaking nearby, is unforgettable. A pleasant restaurant at the hotel serves breakfast (COP$6,000), lunch (COP$15,000), and dinner (COP$15,000). The fare is mostly seafood (lobster is a favorite but will cost extra), but they can accommodate vegetarians.

The Hospedaje Jarrinapi (cell tel. 310/366-4245 or 311/683-4281, www.jarrinapi.com, COP$12,000 hammock, COP$35,000 pp) is a large hotel with 19 *yotojoro* cabins for a total capacity of 60 people. This hotel has electricity 24 hours a day and has a nice, orderly kitchen and restaurant. Posada Pujurú (cell tel. 300/279-5048, http://posadapujuru.blogspot.com, COP$20,000 hammock, COP$50,000 bed) has 14 rooms and a space for hammocks. Pujurú is next to a kite-surfing school.

Getting There

From Riohacha, shared taxis ply the route to Uribia (COP$15,000, 1 hr.). Catch these at the intersection of Calle 15 and Carrera 5. Ask the driver to drop you off at the spot where passenger trucks depart for Cabo de la Vela and intermediate *rancherías*. Trucks make this route, from Uribia to Cabo de la Vela (COP$15,000, 2 hrs. or more). These trucks depart until 2pm every day. The uncomfortable ride on a bench in the back of the truck can take several hours, depending on how many stops are made, but this is the Guajira way to go.

PUNTA GALLINAS

Punta Gallinas is a settlement on a small peninsula jutting into the Caribbean at the very northernmost tip of the South American continent. It is home to about 100 Wayúu who claim this beautiful spot as their ancestral land. The landscape here is a symphony of oranges, ochres, and browns, dotted with cactus and shrubs. The peninsula is hemmed in to the south by Bahía Hondita, a large bay with bright aquamarine waters and thin clusters of mangroves, and to the north by the deep blue Caribbean.

Activities in and around Punta Gallinas include a visit to the *faro* (lighthouse), which is the northernmost tip of South America; canoe rides in Bahía Hondita to see flamingos and mangroves; or visits to two spectacular beaches. These are the remote and unspoiled beaches at Dunas de Taroa (Taroa dunes), where windswept and towering sand dunes

drop abruptly some 30 meters into the sea, and at Punta Aguja, at the southwest tip of the peninsula of Punta Gallinas. These excursions are included in tour prices. If you are on your own, hotels charge around COP$20,000 per person to see the dunes (five-person minimum), COP$150,000 for a group boat ride on the Bahía Hondita to spy on flamingos, and COP$20,000 per person to go to Punta Aguja (five-person minimum).

There are two good lodging options in Punta Gallinas, both with splendid views of the Bahía Hondita. Hospedaje Luzmila (Punta Gallinas, cell tel. 312/626-8121 or 312/647-9881, COP$20,000 hammock, COP$30,000 bed pp) has 10 *cabañas* with 20 beds and is spread out alongside the bay. Breakfast (COP$5,000), lunch (COP$15,000), and dinner (COP$15,000) are served in the restaurant. Lobster dishes cost extra.

Donde Alexandra (Punta Gallinas, cell tel. 313/512-7830 or 318/760-8501, COP$12,000-20,000 hammock, COP$30,000 bed pp) has 10 rooms and 25 beds. Meals are not included in the prices but are usually around COP$6,000 for breakfast, COP$15,000 for lunch, and COP$15,000 for dinner, unless you order lobster (COP$45,000). Donde Alexandra has sweeping vistas of the bay and beyond from the restaurant area.

Getting There

Although most travelers visit Punta Gallinas on an organized tour, it is possible to travel on your own from the Puerto de Pescadores at Puerto Bolívar on a *lancha* (boat) arranged by Hospedaje Luzmilla or Donde Alexandra (COP$100,000 pp round-trip, minimum 5 passengers). In the rainy season, from September to November, this may be the only option.

PARQUE NACIONAL NATURAL MACUIRA

The remote Parque Nacional Natural Macuira (PNN Macuira, 260 km northeast of Riohacha, cell tel. 311/688-2362, macuira@parquesnacionales.gov.co, 8am-6pm, free) covers an area of 25,000 hectares and encompasses the entire Serranía de la

© ANDREW DIER

The northernmost point in South America is Punta Gallinas.

Macuira (Macuira Mountain Range), an isolated mountainous outcrop at the northeastern tip of the Guajira Peninsula. These mountains are a biological island in the middle of the surrounding desert. The Macuira range, which is 35 kilometers (22 miles) long and 864 meters (2,835 feet) at its highest point (Cerro Palua), captures moisture-laden winds from the sea that nourish a unique low-elevation tropical cloud forest teeming with ferns, orchids, bromeliads, and moss. At lower elevations,

there are tropical dry forests. The park includes 350 species of plants, 140 species of birds (17 endemic), and more than 20 species of mammals. The park is within the large Alta Guajira Wayúu Reservation. In the lower parts of the range, within the park, live many Wayúu families who raise goats and grow corn and other subsistence crops.

The gateway to the park is the Wayúu town of Nazareth. Visitors are required to register at the PNN Macuira Park Office, where they must hire an authorized guide (a good idea anyhow, since the trails are not marked). There are various hikes varying 1.5-6 hours, and the cost of a guided walk per group of eight ranges COP$35,000-45,000. Day hikes meander along river beds through tropical dry forest, leading to different destinations. One leads to the Arewolü Sand Dunes, which are, surprisingly, located in the midst of the forest. Another takes you to the Shipanoü pools. A third hike goes to Cerro Tojoro, which affords beautiful views of the coast and the mountain range. There is also a hike along the entire length of the range. If you can, plan to hike early in the morning to increase your chances of seeing birds and other wildlife. Unfortunately for visitors, hiking to the Macuira's unusual cloud forest is not permitted by the Wayúu.

There are bare-bones lodging options in town. One suitable option is Hospedaje Vía Manaure (entrance to town, cell tel. 314/552-5513, COP$15,000 hammock), which has a capacity of 50.

There is no public transportation to Nazareth.

CARTAGENA

Western Caribbean Coast

The portion of the Caribbean coast that stretches west from Cartagena, down to the Golfo de Urabá, and then juts north through the Darien Gap and the border with Panama is less visited and less familiar than the coastal region to the east. That may be just the ticket for those yearning to explore the undiscovered and escape the crowds.

The Golfo de Morrosquillo is home to the beach towns of Tolú and Coveñas, which have long been popular family getaways. Just north of the gulf, the Islas de San Bernardo are where you'll find the world's most densely populated island, tiny Santa Cruz del Islote. Other nearby attractions include the inland town of San Antero, known throughout Colombia for its Festival del Burro, and, farther southwest, the quiet and peaceful retreat Reserva Natural Viento Solar in the community of Río Cedro. This is a place to truly disconnect from the world, and it's only accessible by motorbike via a dirt path.

Across the Golfo de Urabá, the tropical rainforests of the Darien provide an exuberant backdrop to the seaside towns of Capurganá and Sapzurro, which are accessible only by boat or plane. The diving sites off the coast and toward Panama's San Blas Islands is superb.

However, what most visitors remember and cherish about a visit to this remote part of Colombia is being submerged in truly wild nature.

GOLFO DE MORROSQUILLO

Largely unknown to international visitors, the twin beach communities of Tolú and Coveñas on the Golfo de Morrosquillo are popular with vacationing Colombian families from Medellín and Montería. If you can afford it, there are several resort islands off the Caribbean coast, such as Tintipán and Múcura, where you can practically have the beach to yourself, especially during the week.

While Coveñas is mostly a long line of beachfront hotels (and an important Ecopetrol oil pipeline), neighboring Tolú to the east has an easy if run-down charm to it. Here you can get around on foot or by *bici-taxi* (bicycle cabs). On weekend evenings, action is centered in the main plaza, but on the weekend, it shifts to the boardwalk, where vendors sell ceviche, bars blast music, and kids play in the water.

One of the main weekend activities here is to take a day-trip tour of the Islas de San Bernardo. These always include a look at Santa Cruz del Islote, the most densely populated island in the world, with one person for every 10 square meters, and a stop at Isla Murica or Isla Palma for lunch and a swim. At Isla Palma, a resort run by all-inclusive operator Decameron, international tourists may be put off by the confined dolphins and other animals. Contact Mundo Mar (Av. 1 No. 14-40, tel. 5/288-4431, www.mundomar.com.co). Tour operators sell this package for around COP$57,000. They are located in the hotels along the boardwalk. They can also arrange trips to the Islas del Rosario closer to Cartagena.

Beaches in Tolú aren't great; beaches at Playa El Francés or to the west of Coveñas Punta Bolívar are nicer. Before a weekday visit, ask at your hotel about the security situation at these beaches. They are somewhat remote.

Accommodations

◖ Villa Babilla (Cl. 20 No. 3-40, Tolú, tel. 5/288-6124, www.villababillahostel.com, COP$70,000) is the best place to stay in Tolú by a long shot. Rooms have no TV or air conditioning. You can cook your own meals here. There is an Olimpica grocery store a couple blocks away.

The Camino Verde (tel. 5/288-5132, www.vacacionescaminoverde.com, COP$160,000 d, COP$240,000 d w/meals) hotel is on the Playa El Francés, a few kilometers east of Tolú, and is a peaceful spot to relax, especially during the week.

🎧 Punta Norte (Tintipán, cell tel. 310/655-4851, www.hotelpuntanorte.com, COP$220,000 pp) is run by a friendly Uruguayan (Punta Norte is most often referred to as Donde El Uruguayo, or "Where's the Uruguayan?") and his artist wife. This all-inclusive hotel is on the tiny island of Tintipán. Rooms are simple and the lobsters are huge! Days are spent lounging on beaches or discovering nearby islands. Bring plenty of insect repellent should you decide to go to this remote island paradise.

For white sandy beaches, warm aquamarine waters, and the occasional calorie-loaded cocktail, go to the luxury resort of Punta Faro (Bogotá tel. 1/616-3136, www.puntafaro.com, COP$535,000 pp high season), an island resort in the Islas de San Bernardo. High season prices are almost double that of off season rates. There are 45 rooms on the island, ensuring that, while you won't have the island all to yourself, you won't be packed in like sardines. Most guests take a hotel boat from Cartagena, but you can also arrive via Tolú.

Getting There and Around

There is frequent bus service from both Tolú and Coveñas to Cartagena (3 hrs., COP$30,000) and Montería (2.5 hrs., COP$25,000). In addition, the airline ADA (Col. toll-free tel. 01/800-051-4232, www.ada-aero.com) flies from Medellín to Tolú, making this a quick, easy, and often inexpensive beach destination. Getting around Tolú? Take a *bici-taxi* (bicycle cab).

SAN ANTERO

This seaside town's claim to fame is the annual Festival del Burro, one of those many only-in-Colombia celebrations. There are burro races, burro costume contests (in 2013 the winning burro was dressed as the newly announced pope, who beat out a Shakira burro and a Transmiburro, a four-legged version of Bogotá's TransMilenio bus system), and parades. They even have a modern arena that hosts all the fun. The origin of the festival is a religious one. During Semana Santa, an effigy of Judas would ride into town on a burro, and

would afterwards be burned for having betrayed Christ. The festival evolved over time to be more about burros and less about Judas.

An unexpected find of undisturbed mangroves and forest awaits at the Bahía Cispatá nearby. An interesting project by Asocaiman (caimanmiranda@hotmail.com) helps in the protection and propagation of alligators and turtles. These creatures were once hunted for their meat and eggs, but today, former local hunters have been trained on the importance of protecting these species. They now work for the animals' protection. You can visit the refuge (tips are encouraged) and take a short tour led by one of the former hunters. They offer different boat tours of the mangroves, which range in cost COP$15,000-45,000. A locally run and quite friendly hotel, the Mangle Colora'o (Vereda Amaya, tel. 4/811-0722, cell tel. 301/203-7071, COP$35,000 pp), is just across the street.

San Antero borders the water and has some nice beaches at Playa Blanca. Here there is a long string of waterfront hotels popular with weekenders from Montería and Medellín. During the week, it's very quiet. The Cispatá Marina Hotel (tel. 4/811-0197 or 4/811-0887, www.cispata.com, COP$123,000 pp) has an enviable location overlooking the the Bahía Cispatá and, on the other side, the beaches of Playa Blanca. The hotel comprises 16 cute, red-roofed *cabañas* as well as smaller apartments. In addition to the bay and the sea, the hotel also has a large pool.

Go eat at 🎧 Pesecar (Bahía Cispatá, cell tel. 312/651-2651, 7am-9pm daily). It's worth the trip to San Antero just for lunch—fresh, very fresh, seafood, at this restaurant with an unbeatable bayside location.

No trip to the Caribbean coast is complete without a visit to a mud volcano. In San Antero there is a large one, where you'll be able to enjoy the therapeutic properties of the mud without bumping up against anyone. Laugh therapy is one of the many treatments available.

Reserva Natural Viento Solar

It's hard to find a place more peaceful than Reserva Natural Viento Solar (village of Río

alligators at the Asocaiman conservation center, Bahía Cispatá

© ANDREW DIER

Cedro, cell tel. 311/312-2473, www.vientosolar. org, students and backpackers COP$20,000 no meals, COP$130,000 pp all meals incl.). This private natural reserve composed of tropical dry forest is on a mostly undeveloped Córdoba coastline near the settlement of Río Cedro, southwest of San Antero.

At this reserve extending over 200 hectares (500 acres) along the Caribbean coast, activities include kayaking, nature walks, bird-watching, swimming, and yoga. Gentle *osos perezosos* (sloths) reside in this undisturbed reserve, and you may also see howler monkeys, boa constrictors, and iguanas, as well as many species of birds. The reserve is run by a charismatic Paisa woman, Elena Posada, who is affectionately known as La Mona.

Reserva Natural Viento Solar is accessed through the town of Lorica, a fishing town on the banks of the Río Sinú. It's famous for its waterfront market. From the Tolú-Montería highway, you can catch a shared taxi (COP$15,000) that will take you to the coastal hamlet of San Bernardo del Viento. From there, Viento Solar will arrange for a *mototaxi* (COP$10,000) to take you the rest of the way to the reserve.

MONTERÍA

The center of Montería, Colombia's cattle-ranching capital (pop. 409,000), has recently been given a facelift, and in the late afternoon or early evening, it's a pleasant place for a stroll. The Plaza de Bolívar is gorgeous and the spectacularly white Catedral de San Jeronimo stands prominently facing it. The Banco de la República (Cra. 3 No. 28-59, tel. 4/782-3382) may have an art exhibit to check out. For a pleasant walk or jog, head to the Parque Lineal Ronda del Sinú between the muddy Río Sinú and the Avenida Primera. This lovely park under the shade of tall trees and with a view to the river has bike and jogging paths, playgrounds, workout stations, an amphitheater, and juice stalls. This is one of the nicest urban parks in the country.

The coolest thing about Montería is the ingenious (and eco-friendly) system to cross the Río Sinú: the *planchones.* These are small ferries attached to a cable that crosses the river as

Reserva Natural Viento Solar

the captain rows passengers across. It only costs COP$400, making it one of the top cheap thrills in all of Colombia. Even though it takes under five minutes to cross, and there's not much need to get to the other side, the *planchones* themselves almost make Montería worth a trip.

Accommodations and Food

Hotels tend to be overpriced in Montería. The Hotel Casa Real (Cl. 29 No. 6-26, tel. 4/782-4004, www.hotelcasarealmonteria.net, COP$173,000 d) is a few blocks from the Avenida Primera and is also close to a police station. Many rooms are tiny with no windows.

When in Montería, one eats beef. The famous restaurants are on the outskirts of town and are large outdoor cowboy-ish places. While you could order grilled chicken, when in Montería, order a thick, juicy steak. Bonga del Sinú (Km. 5 Vía Cereté, tel. 5/786-0085, www.labongadel-sinu.com, noon-11pm Mon.-Sat. and noon-9pm Sun., COP$22,000) doesn't disappoint its hungry

patrons. Along the Avenida Primera are several bars and outdoor restaurants, and the volume kicks up a notch or two on Saturday nights. In a nod to the significant Arab immigration in the area, Montería has a couple of spots where kibbe trumps steaks. Try Farah Delicias Arabes (Cra. 6 No. 60-42, tel. 4/789-9680, www.farahdeliciasar-abes.com, 4:30pm-10:30pm daily, COP$15,000), an authentic Lebanese restaurant. There is also a Juan Valdez Café (Cl. 44 No. 10-139, tel. 4/785-1607) at the Alamedas del Sinú shopping mall. Get your macchiato fix here because you're a long way from another decent cup of joe!

CAPURGANÁ AND SAPZURRO

The sparsely populated Darien Gap, a 160-ki-lometer-long (100-mile-long) and 50-kilome-ter-wide (30-mile-wide) stretch of mountainous jungle and swamp extending from Panama to Colombia, has long captured the imagination of adventurers. The two crescent-shaped villages of Capurganá and Sapzurro, built between the sea and the interior mountains of the small and low Darien Mountain Range, are within howling dis-tance of the Panamanian border, but they seem far, far away from anything else. Capurganá and Sapzurro are on the eastern edges of the Darien Gap, a stretch of land that connects Central America (via Panama) with South America (via Colombia). The stretch of tropical rainforest here is the only interruption in the famous Pan-American Highway, which extends from Alaska to Patagonia.

With its absence of roads and the cover pro-vided by the jungle's canopy, the entire Darien region has been a major corridor for the traffick-ing of illegal drugs from Colombia into Central America, which has also meant that there has been a heavy presence of both guerrillas and paramilitaries. Capurganá and Sapzurro suffered greatly from drug-related violence during the 1990s and early 2000s. Thanks in part to a strong military presence, safety in the area has vastly im-proved. Though drug trafficking continues deep

the wild, rocky coast of Carpurganá

in the jungle, kidnappings and violent skirmishes don't affect locals or visitors.

While much of the Colombian Darien is lowland and swamp, as it is part of the Río Atrato basin, near the border with Panama, the terrain is mountainous and covered in tropical jungle. Within minutes of leaving your hotel you'll be surrounded by the sounds of the jungle, accompanied only by the occasional bright green and black speckled toad and maybe a band of howler monkeys.

Here in the Colombian Darien, the majority of the population is Afro-Colombian. Capurganá is the larger village of the two, though both are tiny. There are no cars in either village. Get around on foot, by bike, or by boat.

To get here, you have to either take a flight from Medellín (to either the Capurganá or Acandí airport) or take a *lancha* (from Turbo or Acandí). Should the seas be too rough or if a general strike shuts down everything (as when we were there), you may just be stuck in the jungle for a couple days more.

Recreation
HIKING

There are several jungle walks to make around Capurganá. These take you through dense jungle overflowing with tropical vegetation and home to howler monkeys, birds, colorful frogs, and snakes. While the walks are short and fairly straightforward, you may want to ask at your hotel or hostel for a guide, especially for the walk between Capurganá and Sapzurro. Guides cost about COP$10,000. Wear hiking boots (waterproof if possible) and a swimsuit underneath your clothes for dips in the water off of Sapzurro or in freshwater swimming holes, and set off in the morning hours to avoid trying to navigate your way in the late afternoon.

An easy walk to make, without the need of a guide, is to La Coquerita (20-minute walk north from town, cell tel. 311/824-8022, COP$2,000), a delightfully ramshackle waterside hangout where you can have a refreshing coco-lemonade, maybe some guacamole and *patacones* (fried plantains), and take a dip in the refreshing freshwater or saltwater pools. There are also some handicrafts on sale here. To get there, walk along the Playa Caleta beach just north of the port, passing in front of the Hotel Almar. Continue along the jungle path that hugs the coastline. La Coquerita is under a kilometer from town, and the path is well-marked. Look out for the black and fluorescent green frogs along the way, but don't touch them; they're poisonous.

There are two ways to go to the idyllic hamlet of Sapzurro: by boat or on foot. The path to Sapzurro leads you through the exuberant rainforest to a lookout point and then down directly to the Sapzurro beach. The hike takes two hours.

To set off for Sapzurro, start at the soccer field, on the southern end of town, and ask the way. Midway up the uphill path is a shack that is the home of a man who claims to protect the jungle, Once you find him, you know you're on the right track. He expects those who pass through to pay him about COP$1,000. At the top of the mountain there is a nice overlook with views of Capurganá and the coastline. The hike is not difficult, but the

a frog on the path to Sapzurro

path can get muddy and slippery in places. Wear hiking boots and pick up a walking stick along the way to help you manage on the steep parts.

Once in Sapzurro, you're a short hike (15 minutes) up to the border with Panama and the village of La Miel. This easy walk begins on the same street as Cabañas Uvali and the Reserva Natural Tacarcuná. The border crossing is at the top of a steep hill with embedded steps. You'll need to show a passport to cross over to Panama. There is not much to the community of La Miel. It has a small military outpost, many young children running around, and a pleasant beach where you can swim and have a seafood lunch or drink.

Another walk to make is to the El Cielo waterfall, a 50-minute walk (about 3 km) through the jungle. It's easy to make and is flat, although you'll have to make around a dozen shallow stream crossings. Bring a bathing suit to cool off in the swimming holes you'll encounter. To get to heavenly El Cielo, set out on the road that runs parallel to the airstrip. Ask locals for directions.

It is possible to walk between Capurganá and El Aguacate, but the path, along the shore, is rocky and a bit treacherous.

DIVING AND SNORKELING

As you'd expect, the warm, turquoise waters off the coast of Capurganá and all the way up to San Blas in Panama make for fantastic diving, and there are over 30 diving sites to choose from. The best time for underwater exploration is from May to November. During those months, visibility is exceptional with hardly any waves around the diving spots. There are coral walls, reef rocks, and caves to explore close to the coastline.

Dive and Green Diving Center (facing the port, cell tel. 311/578-4021 or 316/781-6255, www.diveandgreen.com, 7:30am-12:30pm and 2pm-6pm daily) is the best place to organize a diving trip (for certified divers an excursion costs COP$190,000) or to take a PADI certification course (5 days, COP$820,000) with a bilingual instructor. For these packages it is best to pay in cash. Credit card transactions will have an additional fee. For those interested in snorkeling, they can help make arrangements for you, though they don't themselves lead snorkeling trips. Dive and Green offers all the equipment you need. If you are on the fence about whether diving is for you, they offer a Discover Scuba Diving day for COP$150,000. Dive and Green has accommodations: four rooms in a house adjacent to their offices. These cost COP$25,000 per person. Although in town, it's facing the water, guaranteeing a pleasant evening breeze.

Accommodations

There are a surprising number of excellent and inexpensive accommodations options in both Capurganá and Sapzurro. While there are a few large, all-inclusive hotels with welcome drinks and the works, the most interesting and comfortable options are the smaller guesthouses and hostels. Nearly all hotels are owned and operated by out-of-towners.

CAPURGANÁ

Many hotels and hostels are near the *muelle* (port) in Capurganá. Here you have the advantage of being in or near the hub of activity. Many visitors stay at one of the few all-inclusive hotels in Capurganá, but those options have zero charm.

The **C** **Posada del Gecko** (Centro, cell tel. 314/525-6037, www.posadadelgecko.com, posadadelgecko@hotmail.com, COP$20,000 dorm, COP$35,000 d) is the best place to stay in town. It's run by an Italian-Colombian couple and offers both dorm and private rooms spread over two houses, with a capacity of 28 persons. In between is a spacious open-air garden ideal for lounging in a hammock or the hot tub. Enjoy a good Italian dinner by candlelight from the restaurant (7:30pm-11pm daily). It's open to non-guests as well, but it's best to go by in advance and make a reservation. The hotel organizes three-day excursions to the San Blas Islands (Panama), in which you visit a Guna indigenous community, frolic on pristine white-sand beaches, and snorkel.

Although there are no sandy beaches there,

outside of the center of Capurganá in the Playa Roca area, about a 15-minute walk or horse ride away, are several excellent guesthouses amid the trees. At night you'll need no air conditioner, and in the morning you may awake to birdsong.

One of the perks of staying at welcoming **Cabañas El Tucán** (Playa Roca, www.cabanatucancapurgana.com, COP$65,000), run by a friendly Bogotana-Italian couple, is that they make their own pasta and are good cooks. This house in the jungle is clean and comfortable, and the prices of their two spacious rooms are reasonable. Right across the path from El Tucán is **C** **Cabañas Darius** (Playa Roca, cell tel. 314/622-5638, www.cdarius.blogspot.com, capurga05@gmail.com, COP$85,000 pp incl. 2 meals), another Colombian-international endeavor. It's a very nice guesthouse in the trees. Rooms are spacious and clean, and it's cool enough at night that you won't miss air conditioning. Balconies and hammocks provide lounging space, but the top selling point is the warm hospitality and Nery's unbelievable cooking. A third option in the same area is **Hotel Los Robles** (Playa Roca, cell tel. 314/632-8408 or 314/632-8428, www.capurganalosrobles.es.tl, COP$85,000 d, COP$70,000 pp). This lodge has quite the entrance—a winding path lined by bright fuchsia ginger flowers. *Caracolí* and *higuerón* trees provide shade and a home for birds. There are 12 rooms in two houses.

The most low-key place to stay in the area is Playa Aguacate. A German has carved a little paradise out of the jungle, and, once there, you won't want to leave. It's popular with honeymooners and those celebrating special occasions. Simple and comfortable cabins, each with a sea view, make up the **C** **Bahía Lodge** (Playa Aguacate, cell tel. 314/812-2727, www.bahia-lodge.com, COP$190,000 pp 2 meals per day). Over the hill from is the lodge is **Hotel Las Ceibas** (Bahía Aguacate, cell tel. 313/695-6392, Medellín tel. 4/331-7440, www.hotellasceibas.com.co). It has three rooms in two houses set amid gardens, and the rooms have pleasant balconies with hammocks for late afternoon relaxation.

SAPZURRO

In Sapzurro, there are also quite a few options. The only drawback is that there are fewer restaurant options. Most hotels offer meals, though, and are usually the best bet at any rate. Cabañas Uvali (cell tel. 314/624-1325, COP$40,000 pp) is a friendly, clean, and straightforward little place in town. It's about a five-minute walk to the beach. La Posada Hostal & Camping (www. sapzurrolaposada.com, cell tel. 312/662-7599 or 310/410-2245, COP$65,000 pp d) has one luxury apartment, with a view, a dorm-style room, and a large space for camping under the big mango tree. They have a little tiki bar over the water, which can be set up for your romantic Sapzurro dinner.

The ☰ Resort Paraíso Sapzurro (cell tel. 313/685-9862, www.paraiso-sapzurro-colombia.com, COP$10,000 dorm, COP$50,000 pp d) has basic beachfront cabins. Free avocados and mangoes is not a bad perk. This hostel is more commonly known as "Donde El Chileno," after the Chilean owner. The hostel can organize oversea journeys directly to Cartagena.

The ☰ Sapzurro Reserva Natural Tacarcuna (on the path to La Miel, cell tel. 314/622-3149, COP$40,000 pp) is a special place for anyone interested in the flora and fauna of the region. Owners Martha and Fabio completed a botanical garden of native species with nature trails and a butterfly farm in 2013, and their other passion is birds. Behind their house up the mountain into the jungle, you can grab your binoculars and wait and watch for birds to make their appearances. Four different types of toucans, cuckoos, parakeets, owls, antipittas, tanagers, and many other species can be seen here. Throngs of migratory birds arrive between August and November each year. The two cabins available are cute, spic-and-span, and of course surrounded by nature. Don't confuse this natural reserve with the all-inclusive Tacurcuna Hotel near the Capurganá airport. They can organize a number of nature hikes in the area and near Acandí.

Food

Hotels are usually the best options for food in the villages. ☰ Donde Josefina (Playa Caleta, cell tel. 316/779-7760, COP$30,000, noon-9pm daily) remains the top restaurant for a delicious, gourmet seafood dinner, right on the beach in the heart of Capurganá. Dining on lobster in a coconut and garlic sauce under the swaying branches of a palm tree: That sounds like a vacation! A decent bakery overlooking the soccer field in Capurganá serves breakfast. In Sapzurro, the best place for a meal is at Doña Triny (Hostal Doña Triny, cell tel. 312/751-8626 or 313/725-8362, noon-10pm daily).

Information and Services

Bring extra cash to Capurganá: There are no ATMs, and credit cards are not accepted in most establishments. To avoid bringing wads of pesos, many hotels will allow (or require) you to make a *consignación* (deposit) to their bank account in advance. That can usually be done from any city in Colombia. The nearest bank, Banco Agrario (Cl. Las Flores with Cl. Consistorial, tel. 4/682-8229, 8am-11:30am and 2pm-4:30pm Mon.-Fri.) is in Acandí, a half-hour boat ride away to the south from Capurganá. To be on the safe side, bring along some extra cash.

Getting There and Around

Aerolínea de Antioquia (ADA, tel. 4/444-4232, www.ada.com.co) serves both Capurganá and Acandí from the Aeropuerto Olaya Herera in Medellín. Acandí is the municipality to which the village of Capurganá is linked. It is south of Capurganá on the Darien. There is one flight per day on ADA Monday through Saturday to Acandí. Direct flights to Capurganá were temporarily suspended at the time of writing.

To get from Acandí to Capurganá, you'll have to take a horse from the airport (seriously) to the docks (a 15-minute trip), at which point you'll take a 30-minute long *lancha* (boat) ride onwards to Capurganá (COP$17,000). There is always a *lancha* at 1pm daily. The seas can be rough at times, so always

Boats are a good way to get around Carpurganá.

try to get a seat in back. You may want to keep your camera or other electronics in their cases so they won't be exposed to seawater. Demand a life vest. The return trip from Capurganá to Acandí leaves at 7:30am daily.

All boats arrive at the *muelle* (docks) in Capurganá, which are in the middle of town. Most hotels are within walking distance, although some, like Cabañas Darius, are a bit of a walk. Try to find someone with a horse to take you there (about COP$10,000). Hotels in Aguacate and Sapzurro are reachable only by taking another *lancha* from the docks in Capurganá, about a 20-minute ride. Those hotels will arrange your transportation from Capurganá in advance.

There are bus links from Medellín (8 hours), Montería (4 hours), and from cities across the Caribbean coast to the rough and tumble coastal port city of Turbo on the Golfo de Urabá. As an alternative to taking a flight to either Capurganá or to Acandí, you can take a 2.5- to 3-hour boat ride from Turbo. These usually depart at 8am,

costing about COP$60,000. The early morning departure means that you will probably have to spend the previous night in Turbo. That's not ideal, but if you must, most tourists agree that Residencias La Florida (Cra. 13 No. 99A-56, tel. 4/827-3531, COP$30,000 d) is an all right accommodations option, close to the port, and the hotel staff is quite helpful arranging your onward transportation.

Do not plan to take a boat from Turbo to Capurganá from December to March. The 2.5-hour journey can be awful during this time of high winds, and the waves can be unrelenting. If you are unlucky enough to be in the front of the boat, you will step off the boat with, at the very least, a painfully sore back. This is likewise true for the trip from Acandí to Capurganá, although it is a much shorter ride.

Returning to the mainland from Capurganá, it's always best to reserve a day in advance for *lanchas* bound for Acandí or Turbo, especially during peak tourist times. Your hotel should be able to do this for you, but just in case, you can call Sara at the *muelle* (314/614-0704).

From Panama, you can take a flight from Panama City to Puerto Obaldía. From there, boats frequently make the journey onward to Capurganá. It's just a 30-45 minute ride and costs about US$15. You may be required to show proof of yellow fever vaccination to enter Colombia.

If traveling onward to Panama, you must go to the Colombian Ministerio de Relaciones Exteriores (Cl. del Comercio, cell tel. 311/746-6234, 8am-5pm Mon.-Fri., 9am-4pm Sat.) the day before for an exit stamp.

SAN ANDRÉS AND PROVIDENCIA

The San Andrés Archipelago is made up of seven atolls and three major islands: San Andrés, Providencia, and Santa Catalina. San Andrés is 775 kilometers (492 miles) northeast of the Colombian mainland and only 191 kilometers (119 miles) east of Nicaragua. The islands are fairly small: San Andrés, the largest island, has an area of 26 square kilometers (10 square miles),

HIGHLIGHTS

LOOK FOR ◖ TO FIND RECOMMENDED SIGHTS, ACTIVITIES, DINING, AND LODGING.

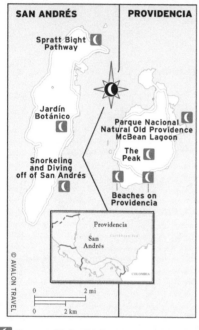

◖ **Spratt Bight Pathway:** Epicenter of all goings on in San Andrés and against a backdrop of the idyllic Johnny Cay in the distance, this beachside promenade is part boardwalk—and part catwalk (page 79).

◖ **Jardín Botánico:** This well-tended botanical garden sits on a bluff overlooking the turquoise sea. A walk among the native trees, plants, and flowers provides a pleasant break from the beach (page 80).

◖ **Snorkeling and Diving off of San Andrés:** The dozens of dive sites among thriving coral formations and steep ocean walls off of San Andrés can keep divers blissfully busy for days (page 81).

◖ **Parque Nacional Natural Old Providence McBean Lagoon:** Paddle through the mangrove lagoons and snorkel offshore among tropical fish at this small national park (page 88).

◖ **Beaches on Providencia:** Undertake the tough field work of determining your favorite palm-lined Providencia beach. Your investigations could take several days (page 90).

◖ **The Peak:** From The Peak, the highest point on Providencia, hikers enjoy fantastic peeks from the jungle toward the deep blue sea (page 91).

Providencia just 17 square kilometers (6.5 square miles), and Santa Catalina, attached to Providencia by a photogenic pedestrian bridge, is 1 square kilometer (247 acres) in size.

Once serving as a base for notorious English pirate Henry Morgan, Providencia—or Old Providence, as English-speaking locals call it—and its tiny tag-along neighbor of Santa Catalina are places to experience how the Caribbean used to be before tourism developed. Here visitors enjoy small bungalow-style hotels and home-cooked Creole food. The beaches are pristine and secluded and the waters are an inviting turquoise.

Seafood, particularly fresh crab, is always on the menu, accompanied by cold beer.

More developed San Andrés is popular with rowdy Colombian vacationers escaping the chilly climes of the Andes. However, it has many of the same charms as Providencia. Sunbathing, snorkeling, diving, and relaxing are always the order of the day.

On both islands English and a Creole patois are spoken, in addition to Spanish.

HISTORY

Little is known of the early history of San Andrés, Providencia, and Santa Catalina. In pre-Columbian

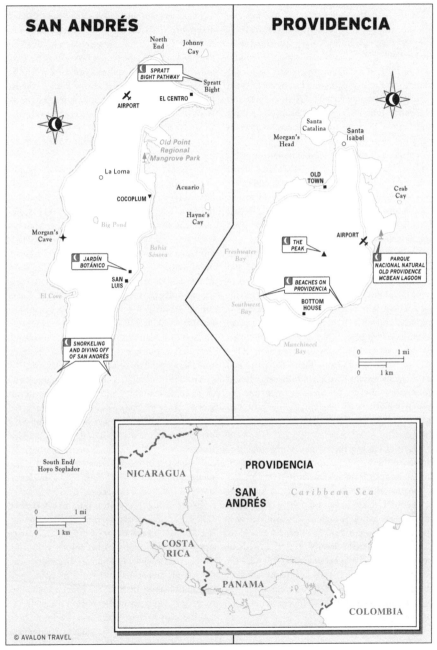

SAN ANDRÉS

North End
Johnny Cay
SPRATT BIGHT PATHWAY
Spratt Bight
AIRPORT
EL CENTRO
Old Point Regional Mangrove Park
La Loma
Acuario
COCOPLUM
Hayne's Cay
Big Pond
Morgan's Cave
Bahía Sonora
JARDÍN BOTÁNICO
SAN LUIS
El Cove
SNORKELING AND DIVING OFF OF SAN ANDRÉS
South End/ Hoyo Soplador

0   1 mi
0   1 km

PROVIDENCIA

Santa Catalina
Santa Isabel
Morgan's Head
OLD TOWN
Crab Cay
THE PEAK
AIRPORT
Freshwater Bay
PARQUE NACIONAL NATURAL OLD PROVIDENCE MCBEAN LAGOON
BEACHES ON PROVIDENCIA
BOTTOM HOUSE
Southwest Bay
Manchineel Bay

0   1 mi
0   1 km

PROVIDENCIA
NICARAGUA
SAN ANDRÉS
Caribbean Sea
COSTA RICA
PANAMA
COLOMBIA

SAN ANDRÉS

© AVALON TRAVEL

times, the Miskito people of Central America visited the islands but never settled there. In 1628, English privateers brought back information to England about the islands that led to the foundation, in 1631, of a Puritan colony on Providence Island, the English name for Providencia. This project was backed by the Providence Island Company, a joint stock company formed by prominent English Puritans who were also involved in establishing settlements in New England. The Providence settlement was contemporaneous with the Massachusetts Bay Colony. At the time, it was expected that this lush tropical Eden would be far more successful than the New England settlements. It was hoped that tobacco and cotton could be easily grown there. In 1631, 100 settlers arrived from England on the *Seaflower*.

The project was short-lived. Providence Island Company denied the settlers land ownership and required significant contribution of manpower to build the island's defenses. Rather than establishing a self-sustaining agricultural community, the colonists imported slaves and established a plantation-based economy. Correspondence from that time reveals decidedly un-Puritanical activity, such as drinking and gambling. The death knell of the colony was the decision of Providence Island Company to obtain a privateering patent and engage in outright piracy. This enraged and provoked the Spanish, the dominant power in that part of the Americas.

Wary of having their New World gold stolen from them, the Spaniards cracked down, and an attack on the islands in 1641 put an end to the Puritan experiment. During the following half century, the island was fought over by Spain and England. Pirates such as Edward Mansvelt and Henry Morgan used Providencia as a base. Nominally under the Spanish crown, the island welcomed a small number of settlers from Britain and other Caribbean islands during the late 17th and 18th centuries. In 1821, the archipelago became part of the newly independent Republic of Gran Colombia.

During the 19th century, another influx of immigrants from the British Caribbean included many former slaves, which led to the creation of the Raizal community. One settler who lived on Providence, Phillip Beekman Livingston, traveled to the United States and was ordained a Baptist minister, and he introduced that faith to the islands. He was also instrumental in freeing the islands' slaves, starting with his own, 17 years before Colombia abolished slavery in 1853. As a result of his work, the Baptist faith became a distinctive part of the islands' culture.

Colombia exerted greater power over the islands in the early 20th century, delegating educational instruction to the Catholic Church and forbidding the use of English on official business. In 1953, dictator Gustavo Rojas Pinilla declared San Andrés a free port. This led to a massive influx of outsiders, mostly Colombian duty-free tourists and settlers, but also a contingent of Middle Eastern merchants, who altered the face of San Andrés forever. A dense shopping district sprouted up on the North End of San Andrés after the declaration of free port. The English-speaking Raizal people became a minority on their own island and lost control of much land. Providence, which was not declared a free trade zone, was spared this onslaught.

The 1991 Colombian constitution gave the islands some autonomy and put an end to immigration from the mainland. Providencia enacted strict zoning and land ownership regulations that have preserved the island's Raizal identity. Both the Colombian and Nicaraguan governments have declared interest in opening these waters to oil exploration, prompting a grass roots "Old Providence, not Oil Providence" campaign.

In recent decades, Nicaragua has contested Colombian jurisdiction over the islands, renouncing the 1928 Esguerra-Barcenas treaty and filing a suit at the International Court of Justice. In 2001, the court reaffirmed Colombian sovereignty over the islands and atolls but left the maritime border up in the air. In 2012, the court decided that roughly 70,000 square kilometers of sea north and south of San Andrés, which had previously been Colombian, were in fact Nicaraguan. Colombians

© ANDREW DIER

iguana in San Andrés

and islanders were shocked, especially because of the loss of traditional fishing areas. Two large atolls became enclaves in the Nicaraguan maritime area. The court decision cannot be appealed, but Colombian president Juan Manuel Santos has declared that it will not abide by the decision until Nicaragua ensures the Raizal fishers have access to their traditional fishing areas.

THE LAND

The archipelago covers 280,000 square kilometers of marine area (it was 350,000 before the 2012 International Court decision). It includes three major islands and seven atolls, and well-preserved coral reefs, particularly the barrier reef surrounding Providence and Santa Catalina, home to more than 80 species of corals and 200 species of fish.

The islands were once covered by forest. Though much has been cleared, especially in San Andrés, significant tracts of forest remain, with cedars, cotton trees, stinking toes, birch gums, and other indigenous trees. The abundance of fruit-bearing trees and plants includes breadfruit, tamarind, mango, and guava, though much of the fruit that is consumed on the islands is imported from Colombia and Central America. There are several large, well-preserved mangrove lagoons, notably the McBean Lagoon in Providencia.

The islands support a wide range of reptiles, including snakes, iguanas, geckos, and lizards, including the blue or green lizard. Other land animals include crabs, especially the black and shankey crabs, which effect massive migrations to and from the sea to spawn. Coralina (www.coralina.gov.co), the archipelago's environmental agency, recruits army personnel to block traffic on Providencia's roads to protect these migrating crabs. Four species of protected sea turtles nest here. Approximately 100 bird species have been identified on the islands, but only 18 are resident. The island's only non-human land mammals are bats. Dolphins and whales are sighted occasionally.

Despite obvious environmental degradation, especially in San Andrés, the archipelago remains one of the best preserved corners of the Caribbean. In 2000, the 300,000 square kilometers of the Seaflower Biosphere Reserve became part of UNESCO's "Man and the Biosphere" program, which aims to preserve both biological and ethnic diversity, combining conservation with sustainable use by local communities. The 2012 International Court decision transferred about 45 percent of the biosphere to Nicaragua. Islanders hope that Nicaragua will continue to preserve this priceless marine nature reserve.

PLANNING YOUR TIME

High tourist seasons on both islands are during the Christmas and New Year's holidays. It may be hard to find a hotel from mid-December until mid-January. During this time, as throngs of Colombian families and a growing number of Brazilians and Argentinians take over San Andrés. Also popular are Easter week and school vacations, between mid-June and August. May and September are quiet. Because it's more difficult to reach, Providencia never feels crowded.

The average temperature is 27°C (81°F). During the dry season between January and April, water rationing can be necessary, especially in Providencia, where it rains as little as five days per month. The rainy season extends from June until November, when it can rain 20-24 days per month. October is the rainiest month and is also when hurricanes occasionally churn up the warm Caribbean waters. March and April are some of the best months for snorkeling and diving because the waters are calm. December and January are windy, making snorkeling and diving challenging. Strong winds can prompt airlines to cancel flights into and out of Providencia.

San Andrés is a possible long weekend getaway from mainland Colombia. However, most opt to stay 5-7 days. Week-long all-inclusive plans are popular. A visit to Providencia from San Andrés can be a budget buster, but it is well worth the expense if you are interested in getting away from it all. A jaunt to Providencia involves an extra flight, and hotels and restaurants are generally more expensive than in San Andrés, which itself is already more expensive than the mainland. If you want to do some serious diving, plan for at least a week, say three days in San Andrés and four days in Providencia.

San Andrés

Surrounded by a large barrier reef, San Andrés is Colombia's Caribbean playground. Here the waters are of seven shades of blue, the sandy beaches are white, and coco locos, the official island cocktail, are always served. Days here are spent lazing on the beach, island hopping, snorkeling and diving, and enjoying fresh seafood. For many Colombians, the deals at the many duty-free stores are too good to pass up—that's one reason why they visit the island in the first place.

San Andrés has a population of about 75,000, about two-thirds of which are of mainland Colombian origin. The rest are English- and Creole-speaking Raizales, many of whom have origins as Jamaican slaves. There is also a community of "Turcos" or "Arabes," whose roots can be traced to mostly Lebanon and Syria. Their presence on the island is not an insignificant one, as demonstrated by a brilliantly white modern mosque that stands prominently in the commercial center.

Orientation

The island of San Andrés resembles a seahorse floating gently eastward in the western Caribbean Sea. It is only about 13 kilometers (8 miles) long from top to bottom and 3 kilometers (2 miles) wide, and has a total area of 26 square kilometers (10 square miles). The Circunvalar ring road more or less circles the entire island.

© ANDREW DIER

The beach at Spratt Bight is full of activity.

The "town" of San Andrés is usually called the Centro or the North End. It is in the snout of the seahorse, in the northeast. This is the center of activity and where the majority of the island's restaurants, hotels, and shops (nearly all of which are owned and operated by mainland Colombians) are found. About 1.6 kilometers (1 mile) of the main drag here, Avenida Colombia, is the *paseo peatonal* or *malecón,* the Spratt Bight Pathway, a delightful pedestrian promenade along the Spratt Bight beach. About two kilometers northwest of the Centro is the airport. The west side is quieter, with a handful of points of interest, hotels, and restaurants. The coastline on the west side is all coral; there are no beaches. At the southernmost point of the island is the Hoyo Soplador blow hole. Continuing counterclockwise, the town of San Luis extends along the southeastern edge of the island. This area has some good beaches, hotels, and restaurants, and is much more laid-back than the Centro.

The middle part of the island, called La Loma (The Hill), is the highest point on the island. The main point of reference here is the stately white First Baptist Church. This is home to the largest community of Raizal people.

SIGHTS
◖ Spratt Bight Pathway

For many, their first stop in San Andrés after checking in to their hotel is the Spratt Bight Pathway (Centro). This pedestrian walkway is the liveliest stretch on the island, lined with restaurants, hotels, and souvenir shops on one side. On the ocean side of the pathway is the island's most popular beach, Spratt Bight, which looks out toward the enticing Johnny Cay in the distance.

Casa Museo Isleña

Casa Museo Isleña (Km. 5 Av. Circunvalar, tel. 8/512-3419, 8:30am-5pm daily, COP$8,000) is a reconstruction of a typical island wooden house that provides a glimpse into island life in the 19th century. After a required guided tour (15 minutes), your cheerful young guide will tell you "now let's dance!" Reggae dancing is a rather strange component of the museum experience, but then again, it's hard to say no. Those smiling guides are a persuasive lot.

Cueva de Morgan (Morgan's Cave)

It would seem that all caves hidden along the coasts of San Andrés and Providencia are reputed to hold hidden treasures stashed away by notorious pirates. On the western side of San Andrés is Cueva de Morgan (Morgan's Cave, tel. 8/513-2946, 9am-6pm daily, COP$10,000), a sort of theme park where Welsh privateer/pirate Captain Henry Morgan allegedly stored some of his loot (but there's no evidence to prove this). There isn't much to see at the cave itself. That's why the park owners added on some reconstructions of traditional wooden island cabins that serve as mini-musuems on island culture and ways of life. You visit these on a guided tour that is included in the cost. One is an art gallery where local dancers often perform to calypso beats. All in all, it's a tourist trap.

Hoyo Soplador

At the Hoyo Soplador on the island's southern tip, the attraction is a hole in the coral where, when the tide and winds are right, water sprays up, reaching heights of more than 10 meters. It can't compare to Old Faithful, but then again, can you order a coco loco in Yellowstone?

❰ Jardín Botánico

The Jardín Botánico (Vía Harmony Hill in front of Hotel Sol Caribe Campo, tel. 8/513-3390, www.caribe.unal.edu.co, 8:30am-5pm Mon.-Fri., 10am-4pm Sat.-Sun., COP$5,000) is easily the most peaceful place on San Andrés. In this lovely botanical garden run by the Universidad Nacional, you can stroll along several paths and view trees and plants that grow in San Andrés. From the five-story lookout tower, you can take in an impressive view of the island and its barrier reefs. Guided tours, included in the price of admission, are technically required, but if you are in a hurry or arrive in the late afternoon, you can request to amble the trails unaccompanied.

First Baptist Church

The white, clapboard First Baptist Church (La Loma, no phone, services 7:30pm Thurs. and 10:30am Sun., COP$3,000 donation requested) was built in 1844 and rebuilt before the turn of the 20th century using wood imported from Alabama. It was the first Baptist church established on the island. A guide will give you a little history of the church and allow you to climb up to the bell tower for a commanding view of the island. The Sunday worship service can last several hours. Church members dress up for services, and you'll often see a smattering of tourists in the balcony on Sundays. The church is an excellent place to hear gospel music.

Paradise Farm

Job Saas, a local Raizal man, operates Paradise Farm (Cove Seaside, Km. 11 Polly Higgs Rd., tel. 8/513-0798, cell tel. 315/770-3904, donations accepted). Saas decided to transform the former standard family farm into one with a focus on

breadfruit at Jardín Botánico

© ANDREW DIER

SAN ANDRÉS

conservation and the environment. Here you can see animals, such as iguanas and turtles, and plants that are threatened due to overdevelopment on San Andrés. Saas uses the same farming techniques that his family has used for decades. It is a great initiative on this island where environmental awareness is lacking. He welcomes visitors to the farm, and, if you are lucky, you can hear his band play.

Big Pond

Managed by a Rastafarian community, the Big Pond (La Loma, no phone, no set visiting hours, donations requested) is a pond on the top of La Loma, home to a few domesticated alligators. When called, they will swim close to the shore, where they are fed a diet of white bread. The alligators live in harmony with turtles, and herons watch the action from a tree nearby. Upon arrival, ask for Fernando. There is no set entry fee.

ENTERTAINMENT AND EVENTS
Nightlife

The nightlife scene on San Andrés is big and brash. The most famous nightspots are near Spratt Bight. Clubs generally open from Thursday to Saturday during off-season but every night during high season. Things get cranking around 10pm. The perennial top discos are Coco Loco (Av. Colombia, tel. 8/513-1047), Extasis (Hotel Sol Caribe, tel. 8/512-3043), and Blue Deep (Sunrise Hotel). Aquarius (Av. Colombia between Bahía Sardina and Hotel Toné, tel. 8/512-5933) is more of a bar scene during the afternoon and early evening, turning into a dancing spot later on. You'll feel like you're in Ibiza at the Majia Restaurante Italiano y Cocktail Bar (Av. Colombia, cell tel. 318/860-5234, www.majiasanandres.com), where chill-out music and mojitos go along with a beachside view. Guest DJs usually spin on weekends.

RECREATION
Beaches

Some of the best beaches on the island include Spratt Bight, near the Centro in front of the pedestrian walkway; San Luis, near Chammey Marina; Cocoplum; Bahía Sonora (near Rocky Cay) beaches; and the Parque Regional Johnny Cay.

Out of all of these, the Johnny Cay beaches are probably the best. Johnny Cay is the island that beckons off the Spratt Bight beach. During peak tourist seasons, on weekends, and on holidays, though, it gets crazy packed.

To get to Johnny Cay, you must take a boat, called a *lancha* in Spanish, from Spratt Bight, It is a quick 15-minute ride there. There are always boats owned by individuals (not organized tour companies) at the ready at the Spratt Bight beach. To arrange a trip, your negotiating skills will be put to the test. Hiring an individual boat can cost up to COP$200,000. The inexpensive option is to take a day tour (COP$20,000). These leave from Spratt Bight by 9:30am every day of the year, and the boats return at around 4pm.

In the late afternoon, the island clears out, but you can stay until almost 6 when the last boats leave. It's nice to be one of the last visitors on the island as the sun begins its descent. There are no accommodations options on the island. While there, take a walk around the entire island, where flocks of birds are likely the only company you'll have. It takes about 15 minutes.

◖ Snorkeling and Diving

San Andrés is surrounded by a well-preserved coral reef teeming with marine life that makes it a diver's and snorkeler's paradise. On the eastern edge is the windward barrier, 15 kilometers long and 60-80 meters wide, with significant live coral communities. Beyond the reef, the shelf ends abruptly with a vertical wall that drops hundreds of meters. To the west, the windward barrier protects a large marine lagoon that has seagrass cover. The reef on the western, leeward side is a bit less well preserved due to tourism and boat traffic, but it also has beautiful patches of coral and significant marine life. In all, the waters surrounding San Andrés include more than 40 species of corals and 131 species of fish. It is common to see large schools of brightly colored

a diving lesson

jacks, tangs, grunts, and snapper, as well as barracudas, groupers, and parrotfish. Other marine creatures include turtles, stingrays, moray eels, octopus, squid, and lobster.

A unique feature of San Andrés is that the dives are very close to shore, which means a 10- to 30-minute boat ride maximum. The water is warm and has excellent visibility year round. The best conditions for diving are January to May, with stronger winds in June and July. Popular dive sites are: The Pyramids, a shallow 4-meter dive with striking anemones and fish; Nirvana, a reef at about 15 meters, teeming with marine life; Trampa Tortuga, a reef at about 15 meters with great visibility; and Blue Wall, on the eastern edge of the windward barrier, which starts at 6 meters and drops to 300 meters with magnificent corals and large tube sponges.

Most dive operators also offer short (three hours) introductory courses for beginners, costing around COP$155,000 per person, which allow you to do an easy dive without being certified. There are also many opportunities to do full introductory and advanced courses with certification. A three-day Open Water Diver certification course typically costs around COP$800,000.

Recommended diving operators on San Andrés include Banda (Hotel Lord Pierre, tel. 8/513-1080, www.bandadiveshop.com), Blue Life (Hotel Sunrise Beach, Local 112/113, tel. 8/512-5318, www.bluelifedive.com), Sharky's Surf Shop (Sunset Hotel, Km. 13 Carretera Circunvalar, tel. 8/512-0651, www.sharkydiveshop.com), and Karibik (Av. Newball 1-248, Edificio Galeon, tel. 8/512-0101, www.karibikdiver.com). Diving excursions typically include two dives and cost COP$170,000. Night diving trips can be arranged by most dive shops.

Other Water Sports

Samuel Raigosa, better known as Chamey, is the kite-surfing guru of San Andrés, and those at Chamey's Náutica (Km. 4 Vía San Luis, tel. 8/513-2077, cell tel. 317/752-4965) are experts on kite-surfing. A one-hour class costs COP$70,000.

park with two components: on the water side there is a restaurant and features include a waterslide, a trampoline, snorkeling, and Aquanaut suits that you can rent to walk on the floor of the ocean. Across the road are some houses made entirely of coconuts, fruit orchards, dozens of lizards and turtles to gawk at, and a cave to enter. South of the West View is La Piscina Natural (cell tel. 318/363-6014, COP$5,000), a low-key spot for snorkeling that attracts fewer crowds.

Tours

The locally run Coonative Brothers (Spratt Bight Beach, tel. 8/512-1923) company offers tours to some of the best known beaches and swimming spots. A standard day tour costs COP$20,000 and leaves at 9:30 every morning. That includes a 1.5-hour stop at El Acuario/La Piscina/Haynes Cay, where you can wade and swim in waters labeled "seven shades of blue." Animal lovers may find the attraction of "swimming with the manta rays" to be disturbing. On busy tourist days, the manta rays are handled over and over again, being lifted out of the water for snapshots with smiling tourists. They are fed a steady diet of white sandwich bread. For the sake of the rays, it's best to avoid participating in this activity. The rest of the day is spent on Johnny Cay, where you can buy lunch and drinks, and rent snorkeling equipment. (If you go to Johnny Cay, don't pay for a guide. There is no need.). You can just show up at the beach at around 9am to join the tour.

Local boaters affiliated with Coonative Brothers also offer full-day tours with more stops, including a visit to the San Andrés mangroves for COP$60,000 per person. There is a minimum of 10 passengers for these tours. If you would like to go out on a private trip to one of those locations, that can cost up to COP$200,000, depending on your negotiating skills. Inquire at the Coonative Brothers' beach kiosk.

Another option to get out on the water is to take a glass-bottom boat tour. During this tour, you make several stops to coral reefs, to sunken ships, and to exotic islands. You'll be able to get

© ANDREW DIER

kite-boarding in San Andrés

The group Ecofiwi Turismo Ecológico (Vía San Luis, Mango Tree sector, tel. 8/513-0565, cell tel. 316/567-4988 or 316/624-3396, 9am-4pm daily) offers kayak tours of the mangroves in the Old Point Regional Mangrove Park led by local guides. The kayaks are completely transparent, providing kayakers with up-close views of sea life such as upside down jellyfish, sea cucumbers, seagrass beds, and also birds such as frigatebirds, pelicans, herons, and migratory birds. Snorkeling is also part of the tour (equipment included). The two-hour tour costs COP$50,000, and that cost includes a snack of a crab empanada and a juice or something of the like, plus a CD of photos from the trip. There are no additional costs. The group also offers artisanal fishing tours, during which the visitor goes fishing with local Raizal fishers. A half-day fishing tour costs COP$200,000 and an entire day is COP$300,000.

The West View (tel. 8/513-0341, cell tel. 312/308-8942, 9am-6pm daily, COP$8,000) is a

SAN ANDRÉS

in the water and snorkel several times to observe sealife. For information regarding these tours contact San Andrés Unlimited (Tom Hooker Road No. 8-75, South End, tel. 8/513-0035, tel. 8/513-0129, cell tel. 316/889-8701, or 310/625-2938). A 1-hour 45-minute tour costs around COP$45,000 per person.

ACCOMMODATIONS

On this island where tourism is king, lodging options are plentiful, except during high season (mid-December to mid-January, Holy Week, and, to a lesser extent, during school vacations from June to July). Top-end hotels and low-end hostels are not as common as mid- to upper-range all-inclusive hotels. Colombian chain Decameron has five properties on the island and is building its largest hotel yet near the airport, expected to be ready in 2015. There are no familiar international hotel chains on the island.

You will probably want to stay on or near the beach on the eastern side of the island, including in quiet San Luis. From here, you can hop on public transportation or hail a cab if you want to go to town, or rent a motorbike, golf cart, jeep (*mulita*), or bicycle. The busy downtown (North End) of San Andrés can feel claustrophobic, but you'll always be within walking distance of restaurants and services, and you can often find some good deals in this area. Waterfront hotels here have pools, not beaches. Stay near the airport if you prefer more seclusion but still want to be close to the action in the city center.

The western side of the island has coral coastline instead of beaches, and the few hotels cater mostly to divers, so this side feels more isolated.

In the interior of the island are some *posadas nativas,* guesthouses owned and operated by locals, many with deep roots on the island. Staying at a *posada nativa* is the best way to get to know the local culture. For a list of guesthouse options, you can visit the webpage of the program of *posadas nativas* sponsored by the Colombian Ministry of Tourism and Ministry of Rural Affairs: www.posadasturisticasdecolombia.com.

In the North End, boutique hotel Casa Harb (Cl. 11 No. 10-83, tel. 8/512-6348, www.casaharb.com, COP$800,000 d) is by far the most luxurious place to stay in San Andrés. The five suites, the lobby, dining area, and spa area are thoughtfully decorated with fantastic art and furniture from Morocco to Malaysia, personally chosen by owner Jak Harb. The Hostal Mar y Mar (Av. Colombia No. 1-32, cell tel. 317/401-6906, COP$150,000 d), in the same part of the island, is a squeaky clean and friendly little place that opened in 2012. There are only four rooms and meals are not included. It's two blocks from the beach. Noise from airplane take-offs may be a nuisance in the mornings for some.

Although it may look retro-Miami Beach, brilliantly white Casablanca (Av. Colombia No. 3-59, tel. 8/512-4115, www.hotelcasablancasanandres.com, COP$391,000 d low season, COP$659,000 d high season) is an upscale option facing the beachfront pedestrian walkway. Of the 91 spacious rooms it offers, 10 of them are *cabañas*. There is a small pool and, more importantly, a pool bar, Coco's. The hotel has three on-site restaurants.

The Decameron chain seems to be on a mission to take over San Andrés. They currently operate five hotels on San Andrés. Close to town is their boutique hotel, Decameron Los Delfines (Av. Colombia No. 1B-86, tel. 8/512-7816, Bogotá tel. 1/628-0000, www.decameron.co, COP$310,000 d). It has 39 very comfortable rooms and a pool. As is the case with all Decameron hotels, all meals are included. Fortunately, you are permitted to dine at other Decameron hotels on the island. This hotel does not have a beach.

The small hotels in the busy downtown are far more reasonably priced than those with a view to the sea and are just a few blocks away. The most popular choice for backpackers is the five-floor El Viajero (Av. 20 de Julio No. 3A-122, tel. 8/512-7497, www.elviajerohostels.com, COP$52,000 dorm, COP$132,000-200,000 d), which is part of a Uruguayan chain. It has several air-conditioned gender-separated dorms, as well as private rooms. The top floor bar serves cold beer and assorted rum drinks, and there are several common areas with wireless Internet and computers. A paltry breakfast is included, and a kitchen is provided for guests' use. Staff aren't overly friendly, but they can arrange excursions.

It's surprising just how peaceful the Posada Mary May (Av. 20 de Julio No. 3-74, tel. 8/512-5669, COP$60,000-110,000 d) is. Every morning you can pick up a cup of coffee in the lovely courtyard that is shaded by a huge avocado tree. On the downside, beds (usually three per room) are on the soft side in the spacious rooms, wireless Internet is sporadic, and in general the place could use an update. Around the corner, Cli's Place (Av. 20 de Julio No. 3-47, tel. 8/512-0591, luciamhj@hotmail. com, COP$160,000 d), owned by Cletotilde Henry, has four double rooms in the main house as well as a *cabaña* that accommodates seven people. You will feel at home here, although the price is high. Casa D'Lulú (Av. Antioquia No. 2-18, tel. 8/512-2919, laposadadelulu.sanandresyprovidencia@hotmail. com, COP$150,000 d) has 10 rooms and three large studio apartments.

Brightly colored Cocoplum Hotel (Vía San Luis No. 43-49, tel. 8/513-2121, www.cocoplumho-tel.com, COP$240,000-420,000 d) in the San Luis area has the most important feature for a beach hotel: It is actually on the beach, with rooms that are steps from the water. Rooms are comfortable and spacious with kitchens. The restaurant and bar face the water, and quite often the only thing you hear is the palm branches rustling in the wind. Food is not fantastic, so don't go for the all-meals-included plan.

Ground Road Native Place (Circunvalar No. 54-88, before the health clinic, San Luis, tel. 8/513-3887, cell tel. 313/776-6036, edupeter-son1@hotmail.com, COP$50,000 pp) is a small, comfortable *posada nativa* with five spacious rooms with air conditioning and wireless Internet in San Luis. It's in the home of Edula and George Peterson and is just a three-minute walk to the beach.

An option in La Loma is Coconut Paradise Lodge (Claymount No. 50-05, La Loma, tel. 8/513-2926, oldm26@hotmail.com, COP$50,000 pp with breakfast), a beautiful turn-of-the-20th century wooden home with six rooms. It's a great place to stay if you are interested in learning about Raizal culture. It's close to the botanical gardens and the San Luis beaches. Try for the top floor room, which has great views and a delicious breeze.

On the quiet west side of the island, for those interested in diving, ◖ Sunset Hotel (Km. 13 Circunvalar, tel. 8/513-0433, 0420, www. sunsethotelspa.com, COP$196,000 low season, COP$320,000 d high season) is a great option. It has 16 bright and basic rooms that surround a small pool. While there is no beach, the hotel's dive shop, Sharky's, offers diving lessons and organizes diving excursions. You can go snorkeling in the waters across the street. Week-long diving packages may be a good option. And as its name indicates, great sunsets are included at no extra cost. You can also rent bikes here.

FOOD

Seafood is on every menu in every restaurant in San Andrés. Fish, lobster, crab, and conch are likely to come from the waters off of San Andrés and Providencia. However, *langostinos* (prawns) and *camarones* (shrimp) often come from either the Pacific or from the Cartagena area on the mainland. A Caribbean specialty you'll likely find only on San Andrés, Providencia, and Jamaica is the rundown or *rondón*. It is a filling to-the-max stew that has fish or conch, pig's tail, dumplings, yuca, and other ingredients slowly cooked in coconut milk. All restaurants are beach casual, and most of the larger ones accept credit cards.

Cafés, Bakeries, and Quick Bites

Part of the Casablanca Hotel, the groovy turquoise Sea Watch Café (Av. Colombia, 6am-11pm daily, COP$18,000) is as close as it comes in Colombia to a New York-style coffee shop. Here you can have a leisurely breakfast as you watch the tourists file by on the walkway out front. They also offer pizza, hamburgers, ceviche, pasta, and desserts.

From the outside, **Coffee Break** (Av. Colombia No. 3-59, in front of Parque de la Barracuda, tel. 8/512-1275, www.coffeebreak. com.co, 7am-11pm daily) often appears empty or even closed. But when you go inside, it's almost always packed with visitors and locals alike sipping on Vietnamese coffee, munching on nachos, or smearing cream cheese on their toasted bagels. Customers here take their time (likely because of the air conditioning!). A bakery/café popular with locals is **Bread Fruit** (Av. Francisco Newball No. 4-169, outside the Sunrise Hotel, tel. 8/512-6044, 7:30am-8:30pm Mon.-Sat.). It's named after the breadfruit tree, which is typical to the area. (There is no breadfruit on the menu.)

Finally, Miss Carmen is a familiar face on the Spratt Bight walkway, where she has been selling her homemade empanadas, ceviche, and cakes for years. Her stand doesn't really have a name, but you can call it **La Mesa Grande de Carmen** (Av. Colombia pathway).

Seafood

North of downtown, the **Fisherman's Place** (Cra. 9 No. 1-10 Spratt Bight, tel. 8/512-2774, noon-4pm daily, COP$20,000) is a restaurant run by a cooperative of local fishers. It overlooks the water and is near the airport, and is always packed. Try the Rondón Típico Especial. Ask anyone in town what's the best seafood place on the island and a solid majority will mention **La Regatta** (tel. 8/512-0437, www.restaurantelaregatta.com, noon-11pm daily, COP$40,000) next to the Club Náutico. It is open-air and juts out onto the water. For a sampling of the finest of San Andrés seafood, try their Fiesta Náutica, which has lobster tails, prawns, and crab. Just far enough for a little peace and quiet from the Centro, **Niko's Seafood Restaurant** (Av. Colombia No. 1-93, tel. 8/512-7535, 11am-11pm daily, COP$30,000) is what a family-run seafood place should be: over the water, not fancy-schmancy, and no lounge music. Lobster is the house specialty.

Seafood, Sustainably

To protect their sustainability, some seafood should be avoided during certain times of the year, and some should be avoided completely.

Langosta (lobster), *pargo* (snapper), and *caracol pala* (conch) are the three most fished species around San Andrés and Providencia, and are very often found on restaurant menus. It is recommended to avoid ordering conch from June to October (but due to overfishing it's wise to avoid conch entirely), lobster from April until June, and *cangrejo negro* (black crab) from April to July.

Other threatened species include Atlantic blue fin tuna, tarpon, lebranche mullet, *robalo blanco* (white sea bass), *mero guasa* (goliath grouper), *cherna* (Nassau grouper), and the masked hamlet, which is only found in the waters off Providencia.

Although the namesake for **Miss Celia** (Av. Newball and Av. Raizal, tel. 8/513-1062, restaurantemisscelia@gmail.com, noon-10pm daily, COP$30,000) passed away not too long ago, the restaurant continues the Raizal cuisine tradition in this cute, colorful, and authentic spot. Located in front of the Club Naútico, Miss Celia is surrounded by gardens and flowers, and the sounds of reggae and other local music add to the atmosphere. They recommend to their foreign guests to only order *rondón* at lunchtime, as they may not be able to handle it at night (it's a heavy dish).

Donde Francesca (El Pirata Beach, San Luis, tel. 8/513-0163, cell tel. 315/770-1315, restaurantedondefrancesca@gmail.com, 7:30am-8:30pm daily, COP$35,000) is colorful and has great food. The menu includes *langosta tempura* (tempura lobster, COP$50,000) and *pulpo reducción al balsámico* (balsamic octopus, COP$34,000). In-the-know locals make a weekly visit to **Restaurante Lidia** (Ground Rd. No. 64-65, San Luis, tel. 8/513-2192) a ritual. It's only open on Sundays and on holiday Mondays. This place gets great reviews from local foodies. Lidia's crab empanadas are recommended.

The Restaurante Punta Sur (Km. 15.8, South End, tel. 8/513-0003, 10am-6pm daily, COP$30,000) is close to the Hoyo Soplador. Sitting on the terrace when the waves come crashing in, it feels like you might be taken out to sea. With a small pool and deck area, it's a nice place to enjoy an afternoon. This family restaurant is a great place for some fresh seafood or drinks. *Arroz con camarones* (rice with shrimp) and grilled lobster are a couple of the more popular menu items.

International

Margherita e Carbonara (Av. Colombia No. 1-93, tel. 8/512-1050, 11am-11pm daily, COP$30,000) gets packed at night during high season due to its prized location near the big hotels. It's a boisterous family-style place where the pastas aren't bad.

Majia Restaurante Italiano y Cocktail Bar (Av. Colombia, cell tel. 318/860-52344, www.majia.co, COP$25,000) is a good choice for some authentic Italian pastas. It's run by a couple from Florence. Mr. Panino (Edificio Bread Fruit Local 106-7, tel. 8/512-3481, www.misterpaninosanandres.com, 10:30am-10pm Mon.-Sat., 11am-4pm Sun., COP$30,000) is a reliable, somewhat upscale Italian restaurant, popular at both lunch and dinner. It's nice to sit on the high wooden tables in the back. Try their *risotto con langostinos,* a prawn risotto that's a generous plate to share.

Although there is a strong Lebanese influence on the island, Middle Eastern food is hard to come by in San Andrés. Hansa Pier (Av. Colombia next to Tres Casitas hotel, cell tel. 313/758-4604, noon-10pm daily, COP$20,000) has a great waterfront location in town, but the falafels and shwarma are nothing to write home about.

It may have an unfortunate name, but the Gourmet Shop Assho (Av. Newball in front of Parque de la Barracuda, tel. 8/512-9843, 12:30pm-midnight Mon.-Sat., 6pm-11:30pm Sun., COP$30,000) is an excellent choice for a break from the seafood platter. The salads, pasta, and other dishes are good, and on every table there is a big bottle of imported spicy Asian chili sauce. With gourmet food items and wine for sale along the walls, and thousands of empty wine bottles decorating the ceiling, it's a cozy place. For something quick, you can try the hole in the wall (literally) Gourmet Shop To Go (Av. Newball in front of Parque de la Barracuda, tel. 8/512-9843, 11am-3pm daily, COP$15,000) in the same building.

Markets

Super Todo (Av. 20 de Julio No. 3-41, tel. 8/512-6366, 8am-8pm daily) is the largest supermarket on San Andrés. It's in the Centro.

INFORMATION AND SERVICES

A humongous tourist office (Av. Newball, 8am-noon and 2pm-6pm daily) was opened in 2012. It's located between downtown and San Luis, across from Club Náutico. Tourism bureau staff are on hand at a tourist information kiosk where Avenida Colombia intersects with Avenida 20 de Julio (8am-7pm daily).

GETTING THERE AND AROUND

San Andrés is served by all the major Colombian airlines. In addition to their counters at the airport, most of them have ticket offices in the Centro. Copa has nonstop flights to Panama City. Air Transat (www.airtransat.com) operates charter flights between Canada and San Andrés. The Aeropuerto Gustavo Rojas Pinillas (Centro, tel. 8/512-3415) is very close to many hotels. Cabs to the airport cost COP$10,000. Satena operates flights to Providencia from San Andrés.

Public buses serve the entire island. These cost about COP$2,000 each way. To get to San Luis, you can take the bus from the Parque de la Barracuda just south of the Centro.

Renting a car is possible, but it's not recommended because parking is scarce, distances are not far, and, more importantly, there are more fun options. Most visitors rent heavy-duty, gas-powered golf carts referred to as *mulas* (literally, mules) for the day instead. Millennium

SAN ANDRÉS

Rent A Car (Av. Newball, in front of the Parque La Barracuda, tel. 8/512-3114) rents golf carts (COP$70,000 day) and *mulas* (COP$150,000 day). Rent A Car Esmeralda (Av. Colombia, in front of Buxo del Caribe, tel. 8/512-8116 or 8/512-1934) offers the same prices. Although you can rent both golf carts and *mulas* for multiple days, their use is prohibited after 6pm.

To take a day tour of the entire island, you can rent a van with the professional and knowledgeable driver José Figueroa (cell tel. 316/317-2020). Taxis are plentiful in the Centro.

Bikes can be rented at Bicycle Rental Shop (Cra. 1B, Sector Punta Hansa, in front of Edificio Hansa Reef, cell tel. 318/328-1790 or 321/242-9328, 8am-6pm daily, COP$45,000/day).

Providencia and Santa Catalina

Secluded palm-lined beaches, gorgeous turquoise Caribbean waters, mellow locals, fresh seafood, and rum drinks make it easy to become smitten with Providencia and tough to leave.

Located about 90 kilometers (56 miles) north of San Andrés, these islands are the easygoing cousins of hyperactive San Andrés. Of volcanic origin, Providencia and Santa Catalina are older islands than San Andrés, and are smaller in area and population than it, having a total area of about 18 square kilometers (7 square miles) and a population of only 5,000. Only 300 people live on minuscule Santa Catalina, an island known as the "Island of Treasures," which was once home to an English fort.

Orientation

The two islands of Providencia and Santa Catalina combined are about seven kilometers long and four kilometers wide (four miles by 2.5 miles). The harbor area of Providencia is called Santa Isabel and is the center of island activity. Other settlements on the island are usually referred to by the names of their beaches or bays. The main ones are on the western side of the island: Manchineel Bay (Bahía Manzanillo), on the southern end, which has some excellent beaches; Southwest Bay (Bahía Suroeste); and Freshwater Bay (Aguadulce), home to many hotels and restaurants. A ring road encircles the entire island of Providencia.

◖ PARQUE NACIONAL NATURAL OLD PROVIDENCE MCBEAN LAGOON

The Parque Nacional Natural Old Providence McBean Lagoon (office Jones Point, east of airport, tel. 8/514-8885 or 8/514-9003, www. parquesnacionales.gov.co, 8am-12:30pm and 2pm-6pm daily, COP$14,000 non-Colombians, COP$8,500 Colombians, COP$4,000 students) is a small national park on the northeast coast of the island. It occupies about 1,485 hectares/3,670 acres (1,390 hectares/3,435 acres of that is in the sea). Here you can observe five different ecosystems: coral reefs, sea grass beds, mangroves, dry tropical forests, and volcanic keys.

Crab Cay (Cayo Cangrejo) is one of the main attractions of the park, and it's an easy place for some splashing about in the incredibly clear, warm waters. This is a great place for some easy snorkeling, and, in addition to tropical fish, you may see manta rays or sea turtles. A short five-minute nature path on this minuscule island takes you to the top of the island. A snack bar on Crab Cay sells water, soft drinks, beer, coco locos, and snacks like ceviche. They are there every day until around 1pm.

Boat tours, organized by all hotels and dive shops, motor around the coast of Providencia, stopping at beaches and at Crab Cay for snorkeling or swimming. These tours depart the hotels at around 9am each morning and cost about

© ANDREW DIER

sailing race in Providencia

COP$35,000 per person. Once you disembark at Crab Cay, you'll have to pay the park entry fee of COP$14,000. Following the stop at Crab Cay, the boats go to Southwest Bay for a seafood lunch, not included in the price of the tour.

Otherwise you can hire a boat for yourself at around COP$350,000 total. Upon arrival at the island, you'll be required to pay the park entry fee. All hotels can arrange this more exclusive option.

The park's Iron Wood Hill Trail is a three-kilometer (1.8-mile) round-trip nature trail along which you can explore the tropical dry forest landscape, and will see different types of lizards, birds, and flora. There are nice views from here of the coastline. You are required to go with a local guide arranged by the parks office (Jones Point, east of airport, tel. 8/514-8885 or 8/514-9003, www.parquesnacionales.gov.co, 8am-12:30pm and 2pm-6pm daily, COP$25,000 pp plus park entry fee).

An additional activity is to hire a kayak and row to Crab Cay or through the park's McBean Lagoon mangroves. Passing through the mangroves you'll enter the Oyster's Creek Lagoon, where you'll see several species of birds, like blue and white herons and pelicans, as well as crabs, fish, and some unusual jellyfish. This is an interesting trip. Try to go early in the morning or late in the afternoon, as the sun can be brutal. Kayaks can be rented at the Posada Coco Bay (Maracaibo sector on the northeastern side of the island, tel. 8/514-8226, cell tel. 311/804-0373, www.posadacocobay.com, COP$30,000). A kayak with a guide costs COP$50,000, and for snorkeling equipment tack on another COP$10,000.

ENTERTAINMENT AND EVENTS
Nightlife

In Manchineel Bay, follow the reggae music down the beach and you'll discover Roland Roots Bar (Manchineel Bay, tel. 8/514-8417, hours vary), which will easily become one of your favorites. It

SAN ANDRÉS

is set back among coconut palms and is the perfect place to spend a lazy, sunny day in Providencia. Or go at night, when you can order your rum drink to go and walk to the beach and stargaze, or hang out by a bonfire. Roland's competition is Richard's Place on the beach in Southwest Bay. Both of these spots often light up bonfires on the beach on weekend nights. Both also serve food, like fried fish.

Festival del Chub

In early January of each year, the Parque Nacional Natural Old Providence McBean organizes the Festival del Chub (tel. 8/514-8885 or 8/514-9003). Chub is a plentiful but not very popular fish for consumption. The purpose of the festival is to encourage fishers and consumers to choose chub instead of other fish like red snapper, the stocks of which have been depleted throughout the Caribbean. There is one area of the island, Rocky Point (Punta Rocosa), where chub is widely eaten, and that is where the festival is held. In addition to an all-chub seafood festival, where you can try chub burgers and chub ceviche, there is also a sailing race from Southwest Bay to Manzanillo. It's fun to hang out at Roland Roots Bar (Manchineel Bay, tel. 8/514-8417) in the morning to watch the sailors ready their boats for the race. This colorful festival usually takes place on a Saturday.

RECREATION
(Beaches

The best beaches on Providencia can be found generally on the western side of the island. From Manchineel Bay (Bahía Manzanillo) on the southern end to Allan or Almond Bay in the northwest, they are each worth exploring, if you have the time. On these beaches, the waters are calm, the sand golden, and there's always a refreshing breeze.

Manchineel Bay, home to Roland Roots Bar, is an exotic beach where you can relax under the shade of a palm tree. Be careful of falling coconuts. In Southwest Bay (Suroeste), there are a couple of hotels and restaurants nearby, and you can sometimes see horses cooling off in the water

beach in Providencia

or people riding them along the shoreline. The beaches of Freshwater Bay are very convenient to several hotels and restaurants.

The beach at Allan Bay (or Almond Bay) is more remote. It's notable for its large octopus sculpture on the side of the road (can't miss it) and nicely done walkway down to the beach from the ring road. The beach area is a public park, and there is a snack bar and stand where you can purchase handicrafts. You'll have to either drive to this beach or hitch a ride on a taxi.

A couple of coves on Santa Catalina have some secluded beaches on the path to Morgan's Head, and there is decent snorkeling nearby.

Snorkeling and Diving

Providencia, which is surrounded by a 32-kilometer-long large barrier reef, is a fantastic place to dive or to learn to dive. The water temperature is always warm, and water visibility is usually 25-35 meters (82-115 feet).

Popular diving sites are Felipe's Place, made up of several ledges with significant coral and marine life; Turtle Rock, a large rock at 20 meters covered with black coral; Tete's Place, teeming with fish; Confusion, with corals and sponges at 20-40 meters; and Nick's Place, a deep crack in the island's shelf that starts at 18 meters and drops to 40 meters. Good snorkeling can be done near Cayo Cangrejo, at the small islands of Basalt and Palm Cays, and around Morgan's Head in Santa Catalina, among other places.

Enjoy the Reef (Southwest Bay, cell tel. 312/325-8207) has snorkeling and diving tours for very small groups, and snorkeling tours for children.

The Hotel Sirius (Southwest Bay, tel. 8/514-8213, www.siriushotel.net) is serious about diving and offers a PADI certification (COP$850,000) that includes four immersions over open water during a period of five days. They also offer a mini-course (COP$185,000), which includes a double immersion excursion. Hotel Sirius's diving courses have an excellent reputation.

Hiking
THE PEAK

The Peak (El Pico) is the highest point (360 meters/1,181 feet) on Providencia, and from this mountaintop the 360-degree views are stunning. This hike takes about 1.5 hours to the top and under an hour down. The path to The Peak begins in the middle of the island and meanders along relatively well-marked trails through tropical rainforest and tropical dry forest. You'll likely come across lizards, cotton trees, and maybe a friendly dog who will follow you up to the top and back.

From the top you'll be able to see the barrier reef that extends for 32 kilometers off of the east coast of the island. This reef is the second longest in the Caribbean and is part of the Parque Nacional Natural Old Providence McBean Lagoon.

To get to the starting point, go to the Bottom House (Casa Baja) neighborhood in the southeastern corner of the island just to the east of Manchineel Bay. Although you may come across a sign pointing towards The Peak, roads are not marked very well, so you will probably have to ask for directions to get to the starting point.

At the beginning of the walk, follow a path straight ahead, veering towards the right, and five minutes later go towards the right before a two-story house. You'll then go left (not to the right of the concrete well). From here on, you will pass a small garden, then follow a rocky creek straight on, fording it back and forth several times. You'll go through a gate and eventually veer to the left as you begin climbing up the hill. After you cross over a wooden bridge the path becomes steep; hold on to the wooden handrails. Occasional signs identify some of the trees or fauna you might see along the way.

During rainy seasons, the path can become muddy and slippery. Make sure to bring a bottle of water with you. Guides are not necessary for this walk, but it's not impossible to get lost. All hotels can contract a guide for you, and this usually costs around COP$50,000.

SANTA CATALINA

From atop Santa Catalina island, English colonists and privateers once ruled, keeping their eyes peeled for potential enemies—usually the Spanish Armada or competing Dutch pirates. Today you can see some remains from 17th-century English rule at Fort Warwick. It is adjacent to a big rock called Morgan's Head. If you look hard enough, it resembles the head of Henry Morgan, the notorious Welsh pirate and admiral of the English Royal Navy who marauded the Spanish New World colonies during the mid-17th century Morgan captured Santa Catalina from the Spaniards in 1670. Morgan's Head is next to Morgan's Cave, where the pirate supposedly hid his loot. You can go snorkeling inside the cave along with the occasional shark. Crossing the bridge, particularly at night, you may be able to spot manta rays gracefully swimming about. Start this hike at the colorful pedestrian bridge that connects Providencia with Santa Catalina in the Santa Isabel area. Once on Santa Catalina, take a left and follow the path.

Tours

Paradise Tours (Freshwater Bay, tel. 8/514-8283, cell tel. 311/605-0750, paradisetourscontact@ gmail.com) is your one-stop shop, offering tours around the island, snorkeling excursions, diving excursions, and fishing excursions. One of their popular tours is the Reefs and Snorkeling Tour (3-4 hours, min. 4 people, COP$85,000), during which you boat to coral reefs around the island, exploring the underwater cities that exist just below the surface. Snorkeling equipment on this tour is extra.

A double immersion diving excursion offered by the same agency costs COP$140,000, not including diving equipment, and lasts four hours. A full-day trip to El Faro reef, nine kilometers off of the island, costs COP$110,000. It's an excellent place for snorkeling in warm, crystalline waters.

On land, Paradise Tours offers several hiking options, such as to The Peak, where you can see coral reefs in the not so far distance; to Manchineel Hill, where you might see wild orchids on your way; and to the Iron Wood Hill in the Parque Nacional Natural Old Providence McBean Lagoon. These cost COP$85,000.

A popular excursion is to take a boat tour around the island. The tours, departing at around 9am and returning at 3pm, make several stops, including Crab Cay and Santa Catalina. Any hotel can assist you in arranging one, and the boats make the rounds to pick up tourists at various hotels. These tours cost around COP$35,000 per person and usually leave from Freshwater Bay. If you prefer, you can rent a boat for just yourself and your crew, but that will cost more, up to COP$350,000. But in this option, you can decide when and where to go.

ACCOMMODATIONS

Located directly over the lapping waters on the eastern side of Providencia, **C** Posada Coco Bay (Maracaibo, tel. 8/514-8903 or 8/514-8226, posadacocobay@gmail.com, www.posadacoco-bay.com, COP$180,000 d) is a small guesthouse with five comfortable rooms, three of which are on the water side. The other two (more spacious) options are across the street. You can go snorkeling just outside the hotel, and you can rent kayaks here, but there is no beach. You will have to rent a golf cart or *mula* to get to island restaurants and beaches.

By far the most luxurious option on Providencia is at Deep Blue (Maracaibo Bay, tel. 8/514-8423, www.hoteldeepblue.com, COP$600,000 d). It has 13 luxurious rooms sloping up a hill. A deck with a small pool provides spectacular views of the water. There is no beach, and unless you plan on dining exclusively at their elegant restaurant, you will need to find transportation to get to other restaurants and beaches on the island.

The Hotel Old Providence (Santa Isabel, tel. 8/514-8691 or 8/514-8094, COP$100,000 d) is the only option in the "town" area of Santa Isabel. It's close to Santa Catalina and offers basic comfortable rooms with air conditioning. Breakfast is not provided.

If you'd like to stay in Santa Catalina, close to the colorful pedestrian bridge is the guesthouse Posada Villa Santa Catalina (Santa Catalina, tel. 8/514-8398, cell tel. 311/257-3054, villasdesanta-catalina@yahoo.com, www.villasantacatalina.com, COP$50,000 pp d). It's a comfortable and clean option and has air conditioning in the room. A small beach is about a 10-minute walk away.

Somewhat far from everything is the ☾ Posada Refugio de la Luna (Bluff, eastern side, tel. 8/514-8460, providenciarefugiodelaluna@gmail.com, COP$170,000 d), a guesthouse with just one very comfortable and spacious room. Carmeni, the owner, is a papier-mâché artist and has her studio upstairs in the house.

The Colombian all-inclusive chain Decameron (Bogotá office tel. 1/219-3030, www.decameron.co) has an affiliation with four locally owned and operated guesthouses in Providencia. These are all about the same high quality: clean, comfortable, and with air conditioning. Decameron requires that you make all of your travel arrangements with them in a tourist package. In exchange for getting the rights to make reservations at these hotels Decameron helped rebuild these family-run guesthouses after Hurricane Beta damaged them and the island in 2005.

There are three Decameron affiliated hotels in Freshwater Bay. The least expensive option is simply called Relax (Freshwater Bay, tel. 8/514-8087, COP$80,000 pp). It has a small pool, hot water, and eight rooms, and is near a couple of restaurants and stores. It is across the road from the beach. Miss Elma (Freshwater Bay, tel. 8/514-8229, COP$180,000 d) has just four rooms and a restaurant on the beach, with each room overlooking the sea. Hotel Posada del Mar (Freshwater Bay, tel. 8/514-8052, posadadelmar@latinmail.com, www.posadadelmarprovidencia.com, COP$190,000 pp d) is a 24-room hotel with air conditioning and a pool. Oddly, instead of a beach, a grassy lawn overlooks the water. Not all rooms have a sea view.

Cabañas Miss Mary (Southwest Bay, tel. 8/514-8454, hotelmissmary@yahoo.com, COP$180,000 d) is beachside in the southwest with five beach-view rooms and three others. The restaurant is pretty good.

☾ Hotel Sirius (Southwest Bay, tel. 8/514-8213, www.siriushotel.net, COP$250,000 d) is a beachside hotel that specializes in diving and snorkeling excursions. (But you don't have to be a diver to enjoy your stay here.) It offers some huge rooms, and the friendly manager will make every effort to ensure you have a pleasant stay in Providencia.

FOOD

Providencia is practically synonymous with fresh Caribbean seafood. A Providencia specialty is black crab. These fast-moving crabs live on the interior mountains and descend to the sea en masse once a year to lay their eggs in April or May. Many restaurants in Providencia do not accept credit cards. Hotel restaurants are open every day, while others often close on Sundays.

The Deep Blue Hotel Restaurant (Maracaibo Bay, tel. 8/514-8423, noon-3pm and 6pm-10pm daily, COP$35,000) is the most elegant and pricey restaurant on the island. However, menu items are innovative and beautifully presented, and the service is excellent. It's a perfect place for a romantic "last night in Providencia" meal, particularly under the stars on the dock. ☾ Caribbean Place (Freshwater Bay, tel. 8/514-8698, noon-3pm and 6pm-10pm Mon.-Sat., COP$25,000) is one of the best seafood places in Providencia. Try the delicious fish in ginger butter sauce or coconut shrimp, and for dessert, the coconut pie. Cheerfully decorated, it is a great choice for both lunch and dinner.

The Canadian owner of ☾ Café Studio (Southwest Bay on ring road, tel. 8/514-9076, 11am-10pm Mon.-Sat., COP$25,000) is likely to be found in this excellent restaurant's busy kitchen. It is a favorite not only for lunch and dinner, but also for afternoon coffee and their trademark cappuccino pie. Café Studio has a varied menu, with pastas, interesting seafood dishes, and salads.

Old Providence Taste (Old Town Bay, to the west of Santa Isabel, tel. 8/514-9028, 11:30am-3pm Mon.-Sat., COP$18,000), on the beach to the west of Santa Isabel, is run by a local sustainable seafood and farming co-op. Each day they offer a different menu, depending on what fishers and farmers bring in. It's the best deal on the island. They can also organize visits to farms and excursions with local fishers.

The Miss Mary Hotel (Southwest Bay, tel. 8/514-8454, noon-3pm and 6pm-9pm daily, COP$20,000) has an open-air restaurant overlooking the beach. It's a nice place for lunch.

For a pizza night, try Blue Coral (Freshwater Bay, tel. 8/514-8718, 11am-3pm and 6pm-9pm Mon.-Sat., COP$20,000). Though not out of this world, the pizzas and pastas here can taste exotic after several days of seafood.

For a midafternoon ice cream fix head to Donde Puchi (Santa Isabel, hours vary). Miss Lucy's (Southwest Bay, on the ring road, no phone, open daily) is a general store, but they also serve inexpensive meals, including *rondón*. It's a friendly, local hangout.

Kalaloo Point Café-Boutique (near Halley View lookout, eastern side of the island, tel. 8/514-8592) is a cute café and shop in a wooden house where you can have a cup of coffee or cool off with a Frenchy's frozen fruit bar. In the store they sell tropical dresses by a Colombian designer and various knick-knacks. There's also a small library.

A small grocery store (open-11pm daily) is in Freshwater Bay below the Hotel Pirata Morgan.

INFORMATION AND SERVICES

There is a tourist office (Santa Isabel, tel. 8/514-8054, ext. 12, www.providencia.gov.co, 8am-noon and 2pm-6pm Mon.-Fri.) in the town area near the port. They may be able to assist with accommodations, including *posadas nativas* (guesthouses owned and operated by locals), and give you some maps. A bank, ATM, and Internet café are in the town. Since 2013, there is free wireless Internet on the island.

In case of an emergency the police can be reached at 112 or 8/514-8000. For medical emergencies, call 125.

GETTING THERE AND AROUND

There are two ways to travel to Providencia: by plane or by fast catamaran boat service from San Andrés. There are three daily flights on Satena (Centro Comercial New Point, Local 206, San Andrés, tel. 8/512-1403; Aeropuerto El Embrujo, Providencia, tel. 8/514-9257, www.satena.com). Charter flights are usually organized by Decameron (Colombian toll-free tel. 01/800-051-0765, www.decameron.co) from San Andrés to Providencia. All flights are on small propeller planes, and there are strict weight limitations. Passengers are only allowed 10 kilograms (22 pounds) in their checked baggage, and each passenger is required to be weighed upon check in along with their carry-on bag, which makes for an amusing photo op. The average weight per passenger cannot exceed 80 kilograms (176 pounds), including luggage. The flight takes about 25 minutes. The airport in Providencia is called Aeropuerto El Embrujo (tel. 8/514-8176, ext. 6528). It is on the northeast side of the island near the Parque Nacional Natural Old Providence McBean Lagoon.

The Catamaran Sensation (tel. 8/512-5124, www.elsensation.com, COP$65,000 one-way) provides fast boat service (three hours) between San Andrés and Providencia. It provides service on Sunday, Wednesday, and Friday during low season. There is greater frecuency during high season. Boats leave San Andrés at 7:30am from the Casa de la Cultura near the Hotel Arena Blanca and leave Providencia from the docks in Santa Isabel at 3:30pm. The catamaran service, while cheaper than air travel, often gets ghastly reviews due to the rough seas and resulting seasickness among the passengers. When the winds are strong and the waters are choppy between the two islands, especially between June and July and again in December and

January, the ride can be extremely rough, requiring boat attendants to constantly circulate among the passengers to distribute sea sickness bags. This is especially true on the San Andrés to Providencia leg. Waters are normally calmer the other way around.

Taxis are expensive in Providencia, costing around COP$20,000 no matter where you go.

Mototaxis (motorcycle taxis) are much cheaper and you can find them almost anywhere. You can also flag down passing vehicles and hitchhike (paying a small fee). As in San Andrés, you can rent golf carts and *mulas* (gasoline-powered golf carts) in Providencia. All hotels can arrange this for you. They cost around COP$120,000 for one day.

SAN ANDRÉS

MAP SYMBOLS

═══	Expressway	◖	Highlight	✈	Airport	⚓	Golf Course
───	Primary Road	○	City/Town	✗	Airfield	▣	Parking Area
───	Secondary Road	◉	State Capital	▲	Mountain	▄	Archaeological Site
⋯⋯	Unpaved Road	✺	National Capital	✛	Unique Natural Feature	▲	Church
─ ─ ─	Trail	★	Point of Interest		Waterfall	▤	Gas Station
⋯⋅⋯⋅	Ferry	•	Accommodation	▲	Park	⤳	Dive Site
─ ─ ─	Railroad	▼	Restaurant/Bar	▯	Trailhead		Mangrove
═══	Pedestrian Walkway	■	Other Location		Lighthouse		Reef
ⅈⅈⅈⅈ	Stairs	▵	Campground				Swamp

CONVERSION TABLES

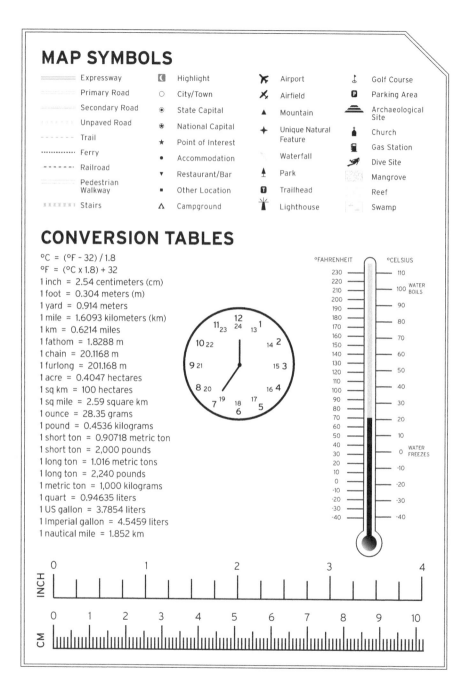

°C = (°F − 32) / 1.8
°F = (°C x 1.8) + 32
1 inch = 2.54 centimeters (cm)
1 foot = 0.304 meters (m)
1 yard = 0.914 meters
1 mile = 1.6093 kilometers (km)
1 km = 0.6214 miles
1 fathom = 1.8288 m
1 chain = 20.1168 m
1 furlong = 201.168 m
1 acre = 0.4047 hectares
1 sq km = 100 hectares
1 sq mile = 2.59 square km
1 ounce = 28.35 grams
1 pound = 0.4536 kilograms
1 short ton = 0.90718 metric ton
1 short ton = 2,000 pounds
1 long ton = 1.016 metric tons
1 long ton = 2,240 pounds
1 metric ton = 1,000 kilograms
1 quart = 0.94635 liters
1 US gallon = 3.7854 liters
1 Imperial gallon = 4.5459 liters
1 nautical mile = 1.852 km

MOON SPOTLIGHT CARTAGENA & COLOMBIA'S CARIBBEAN COAST

Avalon Travel
a member of the Perseus Books Group
1700 Fourth Street
Berkeley, CA 94710, USA
www.moon.com

Editor: Leah Gordon
Series Manager: Kathryn Ettinger
Copy Editor: Deana Shields
Graphics and Production Coordinator: Domini Dragoone
Cover Design: Faceout Studios, Charles Brock
Moon Logo: Tim McGrath
Map Editor: Mike Morgenfeld
Cartographer: Stephanie Poulain

ISBN-13: 978-1-63121-098-3

All recommendations, including those for sights, activities, hotels, restaurants, and shops, are based on each author's individual judgment. We do not accept payment for inclusion in our travel guides, and our authors don't accept free goods or services in exchange for positive coverage.

Although every effort was made to ensure that the information was correct at the time of going to press, the author and publisher do not assume and hereby disclaim any liability to any party for any loss or damage caused by errors, omissions, or any potential travel disruption due to labor or financial difficulty, whether such errors or omissions result from negligence, accident, or any other cause.

ABOUT THE AUTHOR

Andrew Dier

Andrew Dier and his Colombian partner Vio arrived in Bogotá from New York City in 2002. It was initially supposed to be a temporary move – a change of scenery for a while – but 10 years and a couple of adopted street dogs later, bustling Bogotá has become their home.

Excited to share his insider perspective on Colombia with others, Andrew is continuously astounded by the natural beauty of the country and touched by the genuine warmth of its people.

Andrew is a regular contributor to *The City Paper*, an English-language newspaper in Bogotá, and has written for a number of publications in the United States. He's also become a deft translator, mostly for local nonprofit organizations.

Castillo de San Felipe
La Popa - View of City
Walk city walls around sunset?
Mercado de Bazurto Tour
Guayabera (Arte y Creaciones)
Emeralds - Galeria Cano, ask hotel as well

CPSIA information can be obtained at www.ICGtesting.com
Printed in the USA
LVOW01s1159300415

436725LV00005B/12/P